Surviving Girlhood

of related interest

Friendship and Other Weapons
Group Activities to Help Young Girls Aged 5–11 to Cope with Bullying
Signe Whitson
ISBN 978 1 84905 875 9
eISBN 978 0 85700 540 3

Cyberbullying and E-safety
What Educators and Other Professionals Need to Know
Adrienne Katz
ISBN 978 1 84905 276 4
eISBN 978 0 85700 575 5

Cyberbullying
Activities to Help Children and Teens to Stay Safe in a
Texting, Twittering, Social Networking World
Vanessa Rogers
ISBN 978 1 84905 105 7
eISBN 978 0 85700 228 0

Working with Young Women
Activities for Exploring Personal, Social and Emotional Issues
2nd edition
Vanessa Rogers
ISBN 978 1 84905 095 1
eISBN 978 0 85700 372 0

Building Happiness, Resilience and Motivation in Adolescents
A Positive Psychology Curriculum for Well-Being
Ruth MacConville and Tina Rae
ISBN 978 1 84905 261 0
eISBN 978 0 85700 548 9

The Big Book of Therapeutic Activity Ideas for Children and Teens
Inspiring Arts-Based Activities and Character Education Curricula
Lindsey Joiner
ISBN 978 1 84905 865 0
eISBN 978 0 85700 447 5

Rising Above Bullying
From Despair to Recovery
Carrie Herbert and Rosemary Hayes
Illustrated by Roxana de Rond
Foreword by Esther Rantzen
ISBN 978 1 84905 123 1
eISBN 978 0 85700 227 3

Young People and the Curse of Ordinariness
Nick Luxmoore
ISBN 978 1 84905 185 9
eISBN 978 0 85700 407 9

Surviving Girlhood

Building Positive Relationships, Attitudes
and Self-Esteem to Prevent Teenage Girl Bullying

Nikki Giant and Rachel Beddoe

Jessica Kingsley *Publishers*
London and Philadelphia

First published in 2013
by Jessica Kingsley Publishers
116 Pentonville Road
London N1 9JB, UK
and
400 Market Street, Suite 400
Philadelphia, PA 19106, USA

www.jkp.com

Library of Congress Cataloging in Publication Data
Giant, Nikki, 1982-
Surviving girlhood : building positive relationships, attitudes, and self-esteem to prevent teenage girl bullying / Nikki Giant and Rachel Beddoe.
p. cm.
Includes bibliographical references and index.
ISBN 978-1-84905-925-1 (alk. paper)
1. Interpersonal relations in adolescence. 2. Bullying. 3. Teenage girls--Psychology. 4. Self-esteem in adolescence. 5. Teenage girls--Conduct of life. I. Beddoe, Rachel, 1978- II. Title.
BF724.3.I58G53 2013
302.34'308352--dc23
2012023142

British Library Cataloguing in Publication Data
A CIP catalogue record for this book is available from the British Library

ISBN 978 1 84905 925 1
eISBN 978 0 85700 704 9

Printed and bound in Great Britain

*To our family and friends,
for all their support and encouragement*

Contents

Acknowledgement

We would like to extend our thanks to Katherine Wickens for giving up her free time and her commitment to completing a series of illustrations, within a very tight time frame, to ensure that our resources are engaging for young people.

Part 1

Understanding Girl Bullying

Chapter 1

Introduction

In recent years bullying has hit the headlines with startling regularity, publicizing shocking stories of student violence, school chaos and emotional distress. While the media contest that bullying has reached epidemic proportions in our schools and communities, it is largely unclear whether the numbers of incidents are rising, or our young people are finding new, more sensational ways in which to hurt, harass and intimidate others.

Whether bullying is rising as citizenship declines, or society is simply more aware of the problem and impact, the issues remain the same: schools and communities are breeding a culture of disrespect, isolation, fear, aggression, indifference and separation. Bullying is unique in its cross-culture influence, knowing no boundaries in terms of location, class, race, gender, age and beliefs. Bullying is as much a problem in the rural school as the inner city workplace.

We now seem to understand bullying far better than ever before, with countless research papers and books published on the subject each year. It is evident that far more schools than ever before are committing time and resources to tackling the issue, with government support. UK schools must have an anti-bullying policy by law, and many US states have introduced anti-bullying legislation, defining bullying in state law and outlining prevention policies for public schools. Despite these advances and the many bullying prevention and emotional literacy programmes introduced to schools, students and parents still complain of victimization, staff report that behaviour management is one of their most time-consuming activities, and an all too-high percentage of students truant and ultimately disengage from school before they were due to leave.

In our work as anti-bullying officers in the UK, we supported countless victims and perpetrators of bullying, their parents and the schools to understand and resolve issues of bullying. We heard numerous stories of aggression, fear, powerlessness, confusion, exasperation and frustration from all parties. As we strived to train school staff, develop policies and resources, and respond to individual cases, we began to acknowledge that issues referred to us where females were both perpetrators and victims accounted for the majority of our face-to-face work with students. Confounding this deluge of need was the complexity of the work: rarely cases could be solved with simple intervention, and often it was difficult to determine whether incidents were to be categorized as bullying or conflict, and therefore be able to identify a victim and perpetrator with certainty. Bullying is defined as *repeated, deliberate behaviour, where a sense of powerlessness can make it difficult for someone to defend themselves.*

While this definition helps us to clarify the nature of bullying and highlights the main facets of it being *deliberate* and *repeated* behaviour, in the real world discerning bullying from conflict – an argument, friendship fallout, or even a physical altercation – can be much more difficult. As we were discovering, particularly with girl bullying, identifying the victim and perpetrator wasn't as clear cut as first appeared, as girls would often become embroiled in retaliation and taking sides. However, this is not to say there weren't many incidents where it was clear someone was on the receiving end of often vicious, distressing and harmful behaviour, which should be classed as a bullying incident and dealt with as such.

On a daily basis we heard the frustration and uncertainty of staff feeling overwhelmed by low-level incidents that consumed their time and rarely seemed to be resolved despite intervention and support. These incidents involved both girls and boys of all ages, on a spectrum from minor disagreements to physical fights resulting in hospitalization. However, the issue requiring the most time and effort to resolve was relationship problems within friendship groups of girls, where girls would destroy friendships with startling regularity, complain of rumour spreading, damage reputations, make verbal comments and put-downs, emotionally blackmail, and exchange 'dirty looks', to name but a few female tactics. The cycle and exchange of roles from perpetrator to victim left teachers struggling to identify any one action as bullying; however, it seemed apparent that these kinds of behaviours were a subset of bullying, and overall, created a climate of fear, distrust, disconnection and cliques throughout the school.

This book and the activities included here were written for the teacher, counsellor, teaching aide, behaviour specialist or educational psychologist who has experienced the demoralizing rollercoaster of trying to help girls make and maintain friendships and avoid relationship issues escalating to bullying.

Our approach and activities are designed to support the overall well-being of girls, address their social and emotional needs, and help to improve behaviour, relationships and learning across the school. As the title suggests, *Surviving Girlhood* aims to help young women navigate their way through what has always been a challenging time, as childhood gives way to adolescence. At a time when young people are subjected to huge pressures, temptations and external stresses, life can feel more like survival. As caring adults we want the best for our children and to see them relish life. Our hope is that adolescence is a time of growth, maturity, learning and fun that builds a strong foundation for the future.

This book has been written to help tackle girl bullying and relationship problems by preventing such issues from occurring in the first place. *Surviving Girlhood* will upskill our young people with tools, strategies and, most importantly, awareness. The five key themes to *Surviving Girlhood* start from the 'inside-out', reflecting a philosophy of understanding and connecting with ourselves, to better understand and connect with others.

The five key themes to *Surviving Girlhood*

- Theme 1: Being Me
- Theme 2: Influences
- Theme 3: Respect, Responsibilities, Relationships
- Theme 4: Managing Relationships
- Theme 5: Conflict Resolution

Chapter 2

A New Way

While it is crucial that we educate our children to understand what bullying is, how they can prevent it, to whom they should report bullying, and the other nuances that empower young people to be able to tackle the issue, it is clear that this is only one part of the picture. Viewed in terms of a model of escalation (Figure 2.1), bullying is a result of lower-level behaviours escalating to create a *culture of bullying* and potentially leading to the formation of gangs, violence and criminal behaviour, sadly leaving a too-high percentage of our young people incarcerated before they even reach the age of 18.

What separates the *Surviving Girlhood* approach to tackling bullying from that of others is our belief that bullying is, in essence, symptomatic. Echoing what appears to be the pervasive attitude of our society, schools reactively deal with the issues presented instead of looking beyond to explore the root cause. Just as a headache tablet may stop a pounding head for a while, anti-bullying education and policies will similarly help to reduce bullying in the short term. Just as our body may be indicating a deeper concern with a persistent headache, bullying is a reflection of deeper rooted issues with a school's climate. Focusing solely on the problem and constantly fighting fires is ineffective and speaks of a need to go beyond the symptom to explore what's infecting our schools and communities with disease.

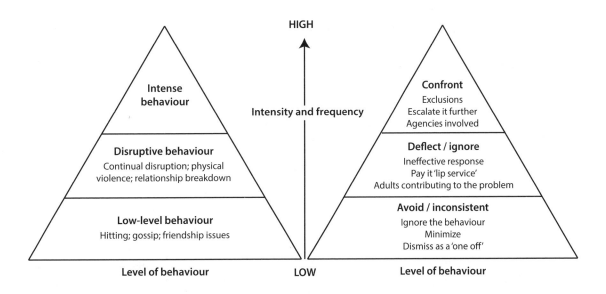

Adults can reinforce and escalate the behaviour with ineffective and inappropriate responses; adult response can reinforce the negative thinking and behaviour of the young people involved without equipping them with the skills to manage future conflict.

Figure 2.1: A model of escalation

A new approach

A war on drugs, a war on terrorism, a war on violence and bullying in our schools – all too often we hear the call to reform society with tough measures and strong action, often well meant but inexplicably ill placed. A war on anything is still, by definition, a war, and a negative, pessimistic approach to advocating change in our education systems.

Research tells us of the importance of adult influence on children, and how children will consciously and unconsciously repeat and re-enact what is modelled to them by key adults in their life. Social Learning Theory, derived from the work by psychologist Albert Bandura, denotes that children learn and imitate observable behaviours, creating ideas for how new behaviours should be enacted (Bandura 1976). This process of modelling and the subtle messages communicated through tone, language and attitude are how we learn what to say, how to say it, how we interact with others, how we use our power and influence, what is important to us (our values) and even our beliefs – the cornerstone of what it means to be 'us'.

Trying to resolve a negative issue such as bullying with negative action, messages or consequence (e.g. the threat of punishment) will always be counterproductive. It stands to reason that what we promote we will see, or in another way, what we look for we will find. Our children are also adept at recognizing the inconsistency of our words and actions when we send confusing and nonsensical messages – threatening children with the fear of punishment for anyone who hurts another through conflict or bullying, for example. As we tell children not to use their power over one another, we demonstrate the opposite – using threatening, manipulative and controlling words or behaviour to make children compliant, typically through fear of consequence rather than being able to choose to do right by their own judgement and will. This is not to say that consistent, measured and appropriate consequences to poor behaviour shouldn't be communicated to the whole-school community. Sanctions still have their place, but only in conjunction with discussion, reflection and exploration of the child's and school's needs.

When faced with issues and challenges in the classroom, it can be a natural response to focus on the problems we see and become caught up with the predicament we are faced with, often in a reactive way. The *Surviving Girlhood* perspective differs in the very foundation of how we approach problems, difficulties, issues and testing circumstances, such as dealing with pervasive bullying. Our focus is simply on what we *want* to see in our classrooms, school corridors, playgrounds, homes, streets and communities. By modelling to children the positive attributes we wish to see and empowering our young people to understand themselves better, we create a powerful chain of self-directed influence, teaching young people the strength of a life lived in alignment with their own positive values and attitudes.

Relationships: The core of conflict and harmony

In a fast paced world, it can feel as though it is 'every man for himself', and we are often taught, implicitly and explicitly, that we need to think of ourselves before others. Our education systems, religious teachings, and cultural and societal influences promote the idea of 'me' as separate to others – what do *I* like, what do *I* want, how do *I* feel? While autonomy is important, the decline of community and overemphasis on personal gratification has lowered the importance of social responsibility and connection to others. The concept of relationship is slowly becoming limited to a romantic partner and a few close friends, breeding a sense of isolation, loneliness, disassociation and a lack of support; or wildly exaggerated to hundreds of strangers we acknowledge as 'friends' on our social networking sites, and with whom young people often share personal and intimate information, despite never meeting in real life.

As we shift our perception to a different paradigm, where bullying is a symptom of an underlying concern, we begin to note the connectedness of the entire school community, and beyond. The actions of the individual contribute to the school climate as a whole, creating a ripple effect of influence. The head teacher can set the tone for the entire staff in the morning meeting; the science teacher influences five or six groups of 30-plus children in one day; and the radical behaviour of the school 'bad boy' flows through the corridors as gossip and whispers, and is then taken home with children and passed through the wider web of connectedness via social networking sites. On a macrocosm level, the same can be said about the world as a whole: never before in our history have we been so technologically connected, hearing about events occurring in far-flung places as they are broadcast directly into our living rooms and offices. As social theorists, psychotherapists and quantum physicists declare, we exist in a web of interconnectedness where our actions, thoughts and feelings affect others, both directly and indirectly.

As we begin to explore the importance of our lives in relation to others, we note how being in a harmonic relationship with ourselves and others provides us with our most basic and key needs – the need for inclusion, support, acknowledgement, fun, connection, safety and growth, among others. Can the problems we see on a day-to-day basis in our schools, communities and across the world as a whole be resolved with a focus on relationships?

When an incident of bullying occurs, or a playground fight, a teacher admonishing a student for late arrival, an argument between child and parent, a teacher gossiping about another member of staff, or a heated discussion about a new curriculum approach, relationships are affected. Those involved may feel anger, disappointment, sadness, frustration and a whole host of uncomfortable feelings, *in relation to another person or persons*. It is extremely rare for an event or feeling to be held in a person's thoughts separate from the context of the person who was involved or who we feel caused the thoughts and feelings we now have. Consider someone who didn't indicate when changing lanes while driving and nearly caused you to have an accident. Does the road rage you experience float disconnectedly through your mind, or is it linked to the other driver, whether you know them or not?

Our failure to focus on creating harmonious, supportive and fulfilling relationships, in addition to our disregard for how relationships are affected by day-to-day issues, will lead to symptoms of bullying and similar behaviours. As the teachers dealing with girl issues will confirm, the damage to relationships with negative, underhand, mean and bullying behaviour cause untold misery and stress. By promoting and enhancing relationships and highlighting the connectedness of all people, we can begin to challenge all members of the school community to develop stronger and more effective relationships and to repair the relationship when damage is caused.

Being in relationship with myself

Developing childrens' (and adults') awareness of the importance of relationships with others is only half of the equation. While we are constantly in relationship with all those we come across and the greater world around us, including the environment in which we live, we are also always in relationship, as a verb, with ourselves. This connection to ourselves is through our inner thoughts and internal voice, our feelings, actions, likes and dislikes, the choices we make, and all the other nuances of our daily behaviour. Our waking life is spent in conversation with ourselves, and our thoughts reflect the quality of our self-relationship. A strong connection to oneself can be defined as knowing yourself clearly; understanding your feelings and drivers; and making choices and taking action based on inner reflection, intuition, and in alignment to inner goals and self-serving desires. Those who are disconnected from themselves, or who cannot discern who they truly are, may experience inner conflict and a confusion that is reflected in transient, conflicted or chaotic relationships with others. The old adage, although a little clichéd, stands true – to truly know someone, I must first know myself.

A school-wide or individualized programme that seeks to promote positive relationships with others must also include a focus on developing a positive relationship with oneself. Too often adults and children struggle to maintain friendships, social and family connections, or romantic relationships because of their inability to relate to, and be in relationship with, themselves. Young women who are supported in developing strong and healthy self-relationships are less likely to be distrustful, abusive or manipulative, and are more likely to be able to regulate their emotions, demonstrate empathy, create strong social connections and live in alignment to their needs and values.

Needs and values

All relationships are essentially an interplay of needs, and arguably all of our actions are conscious and unconscious techniques to meet our needs. The prominent psychologist Abraham Maslow defined basic human needs as survival, protection/safety, belonging, competence/learning, and autonomy or self-actualization (Maslow 1943), but the list of non-basic needs is endless. Each of us may have a list of key needs based on our personalities and our values (the things that are most important to us) that we strive to fulfil on a daily basis, whether we are conscious of it or not. This may be a need for organization and to be ordered, a need for control or power, a need for adventure and autonomy – the list is inexhaustible and unique to each person. Consider what may be important to you and how this is reflected in your daily life. Noting how our needs are met, or are not being met, may give us clues to where we seek satisfaction in life and where conflicts may be occurring. For example, a person with a need for order and control may feel extremely uncomfortable and conflicted working in a chaotic, ever-changing and disorganized office.

Our children come to school with a long list of needs, and for some not even basic needs of protection and survival (having clean clothes, adequate warmth and nutritious food) are being fulfilled at home. Entering a place where they are expected to concentrate and learn in an already needy state is clearly a recipe for disaster, as we often see with children who truant, have difficulty concentrating, or cause behavioural disruptions. For other children, less obvious but nonetheless crucial needs go unfulfilled, such as a need for connection, belonging or attention. Regardless of whether parents and home life provide basic needs, children, like all of us, will still need affection, interest, fun, growth, learning – all of which can be fulfilled by teachers, other students, and through the learning process.

While having needs is completely natural, complications arise when we are unaware of our needs or seek to meet them in unhealthy or unresourceful ways. Consider the young woman who meets her need for attention and appreciation by dressing provocatively, or the young man who strives to meet his needs for connection and acceptance by displaying aggressive behaviour and joining a violent gang. Education and awareness-raising about needs may be particularly crucial for young women who may be at risk of trying to meet their needs in ways which lead to sexual promiscuity, early pregnancy, bullying, alcohol and drug abuse, or domestic abuse in romantic relationships.

Understanding the needs of the individual reminds us of the importance of being aware of the needs of the whole – in this case the whole-school community. By focusing on individual needs, we are better placed to consider the needs of the collective, which this programme strives to achieve. A person, group or community whose needs are fully met are then in a stronger position to seek to meet the needs of others. As members of the school community begin to feel supported, listened to and connected, rather than disparate and disconnected, people can come together to solve wider issues and to contribute to solutions, rather than problems. Understanding and meeting our needs also allows us to consider what is important to us and to create a life that reflects our innermost values. On a collective level, the school reflects the values of all its members when they work together to meet each other's needs in positive, resourceful ways.

As you may note, the activities and worksheets included here do not focus much on bullying, despite our overall aim of reducing girl bullying. Instead, our focus is on encouraging and developing girls' emotional and social awareness by focusing on meeting their needs and living their values in a positive, constructive manner. The activities promote the competencies we all wish to see in our schools and communities, which naturally lead to a reduction in relationship issues, bullying, aggression and violence across the school. The lessons learned are, in fact, a shift in awareness, as girls begin to understand themselves and others better. These 'life lessons' foster empathy, emotional literacy, social skills, conflict resolution skills and, most importantly, self-esteem and self-acceptance.

Chapter 3

Girl Friendships and Girl Bullying

The Facts

As any parent or teacher will know, the very natures of girls' friendships are complex and can be difficult to understand. The social nature of women, more so than men, can lead to girls forming tight-knit groups of friends in addition to, or instead of, a best friend, driven by their need for social interaction and acceptance. A role in a group can provide a sense of connection and protection but can also lead to dissonance and conflict when the needs of individuals in the group differ or members seek to meet their needs in unhealthy or unresourceful ways. For many girls, friendships are the centre of their world, whether they are positive relationships or not. Girls' relationships are marked by intimacy as young women look to their friends for social, emotional and physical support. Girls will talk about feelings and issues, be emotional, and share secrets and gossip to a greater extent than boys, whose relationships are far more fluid and detached.

Research states that during early adolescence girls grow in self-consciousness, becoming more concerned with how they are received and liked by others. Their desire to achieve decreases as their desire to be well liked increases, affecting girls' confidence and self-esteem as well as their self-perception. Adolescent girls become increasingly people-oriented, while boys are more concerned with achievement (Rosenburg and Simmons 1975).

When things go wrong in female relationships, girls have a greater tendency to internalize thoughts and feelings, ruminating on the problem and creating patterns of thinking that can become exaggerated and disproportionately negative. Negative thoughts can fester and dominate a person's perspective until they are owned and are accepted as fact. The girl who hears a rumour about her appearance can quickly create an exaggerated perception of how others view her, amplifying the original comment to gargantuan proportions and internalizing the results as her own beliefs, thereby believing herself to be unstylish, ugly, unwanted, or the like. The thoughts, if repeated enough, become beliefs, which in turn can become externalized as behaviours, as the girl who believes others think of her as ugly lashes out with words or fists to communicate her pain or retaliate for the hurt she feels. The recipient of such behaviour may be shocked at the depth of feeling elicited by such a seemingly innocent comment. Teachers and parents should be particularly aware of the strength of internalized beliefs and their impact on behaviour: many teachers will have experienced out of character behaviour or a reaction from a child that is completely disproportionate to the event, as a negative perception, belief or pattern of thinking is triggered. Girls particularly are more likely to engage in relationally aggressive behaviours as a result of internalized thoughts and beliefs than boys, who employ physically aggressive actions instead. This behaviour may include destroying other girls' relationships; damaging reputations; engaging in manipulation, such as coercing others into self-serving action; encouraging others to take sides; and using tactics such as gossip spreading, cyber bullying and verbal put-downs.

The strong need for connection and approval through social connections and from peers can keep girls returning to the same group of friends after an incident of conflict or bullying, only for the cycle to begin again in a sequence of repetition that leaves adults exasperated and confused, as demonstrated in Figure 3.1. For the victim on the receiving end of bullying or relationally aggressive behaviour, the need to be included in the group and the desire to maintain social links will see them returning to the circle or continually engaging with the protagonist in a push-and-pull scenario, where others are encouraged to take sides and stake their support for one girl or the other. The victim of such behaviour might also be aware that she may be safer in the group than outside it, as she can employ her own relationally aggressive behaviours to target someone else as the victim next time, leaving her safe from the line of fire. This fluid, ever-changing dynamic of female relationships speaks of the difficulty in identifying a clear victim and perpetrator and understanding the roles of the other members of the group. While there may often be a 'Queen Bee' of a group who leads and directs the dramas that unfold around her, her actions may be so subtle or manipulative that it becomes hard to account the situation to her behaviour. Similarly, the victims, messengers and bystanders may be hard to define, as the web of 'who did what to whom' becomes unendingly tangled.

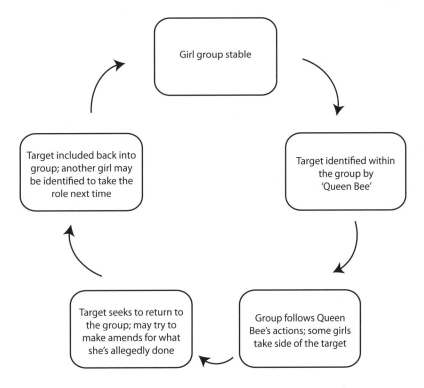

Figure 3.1: The cycle of relationship dramas

This inauthentic and messy cycle of friendships can have far-reaching consequences. The tactics, behaviours and beliefs that girls learn in childhood and adolescence stay with them into adulthood, becoming a model for how to parent and raise their own children, as well as interact with friends, family and a spouse in later life. Girls who believe that love is subservience, or who learn that power is control, and that control is gained by violence and aggression, will undoubtedly model these behaviours to their own children in the future. Girls whose relationships are fraught with anxiety, dominance, abuse and power struggles will likely create romantic relationships of the same nature and struggle to break free to experience more authentic relationships, seemingly meeting the same kind of partner over and over again as their beliefs and expectations for relationships are mirrored in the characteristics of their partner, however unproductive and unhealthy they may be. This succession of poor friendship behaviours to girl bullying and relational aggression, poor romantic relationships and parenting, as depicted in Figure 3.2, describes the ongoing cycle that our schools, communities and society as a whole will have to manage for generations to come, unless girls are supported to seek a new way to meet their needs and develop healthy connections with others. Education and support for boys is also key: as girls are supported to better understand their needs and values, and to build authentic relationships, so too must boys be educated about the constructs of a positive, healthy romantic or sexual relationship, and how to meet their needs while meeting those of their partners. Common stereotypes and cultural perceptions that boys must be seen to be strong, hiding their feelings and playing a role of dominance and control, is just as unhelpful and important to explore.

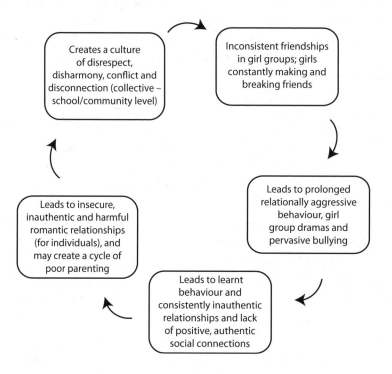

Figure 3.2: An ongoing cycle

For many girls the concept of friendship is a saccharine ideal – friends are trustworthy, supportive and fun. In reality, many young people fail to see the connection between their own behaviour and the notion of themselves as a friend, and are unaware of the damaging methods they use to meet their social needs through friendships. Many young women may make connections with others not based on a mutual care, bond or shared interest, but on a perceived sense of social status or protection from bullying or relational conflict – the notion that it safer to be 'friends' with the school bully, than not. The alarming trend of creating exaggerated numbers of virtual connections also muddies the waters of appropriate friendly behaviour and interaction. While most girls can link the idea of a friend to those they spend time with in school or in their neighbourhood, the birth of social networking, Internet-ready phones and interactive gaming has expanded the concept of friendship to become a blanket ideal for almost anyone, whether they are known in the real world, or not. A report published by the Kaiser Family Foundation in 2010 suggested that on average 40 per cent of boys and girls aged 8–18 are likely to visit social networking sites in a typical day and girls are likely to remain on those sites for over an hour. A survey conducted in 2011 by the consumer research group Intersperience found that teenagers aged 13–16 average 450 people as their 'friends' or contacts on their social networking sites, a number they are highly unlikely to know in a face-to-face capacity (Intersperience Research 2011).

While expanded social connection is now a reality that can bring many benefits, the dangers of allowing young people open and free access to the Internet, representing a potential connection to billions of people, are sadly all too real for young victims of cyber bullying, cyber stalking, identity theft, online harassment and, in extreme cases, sexual abuse and paedophilia.

The needy, manipulative and socially promiscuous behaviour of some young women is a dangerous recipe for unwanted and destructive contact, either in the real or virtual world. While we strive to educate our young people about bullying, it is clear that we need to also develop their social skills, social responsibility and inner awareness of what it means to be a friend. Equally concerning, young people's sense of privacy is far different nowadays than that of older generations, as children and teenagers are accustomed to leaving a virtual footprint on the World Wide Web, opening the way for potential identity crimes, the theft of personal information and a trail of traceable data, including images and video, that young people may rather forget as they grow older.

Cyber bullying

Cyber bullying is the bullying of a person or persons through the use of technology such as mobile phones and the Internet. The explosion of the Internet, particularly social networking sites, and the availability of personal computers and mobile devices with web connectivity have simultaneously expanded our world to new possibilities and opened the floodgates of opportunity for bullying, harassment, cruelty and criminal activity.

As countless research studies have found, the level of cyber bullying has steadily increased since the birth of common access to technology, with young women in particular claiming to be the victim of such behaviour. There are seven types of cyber bullying: bullying via text message, phone call, email, Instant Messenger (IM, e.g. MSN), websites (including social networking sites), video and pictures (on phones, cameras, posting images on the web) and through Internet chat rooms.

Cyber bullying may be more difficult to label and define than more traditional forms, and the debate rolls on as to whether a, theoretically speaking, 'single' incident (such as posting a nasty comment on a person's social networking site) is bullying or not, primarily because the comment is repeated by the nature of it being displayed on multiple people's computers and possibly being commented upon by multiple people. It is, in essence, still a single act and not repeated by the perpetrator, as the definitions used to categorize behaviours as bullying describe. These acts, whether bullying or cyber harassment, can encourage negative bystander action as others are tempted to write a comment online or forward a picture or text message. The physical distance between victim and perpetrator can create a disconnection from the true impact of the behaviour: the remorse and empathy that may be elicited by seeing another person in pain is often removed when the impact is distanced.

By the nature of cyber bullying, evidence of an attack is easier to collect as victims can print emails, save text messages or copy online conversations as they occur. Similarly, defending oneself from subsequent attacks can be as easy as blocking an email address or contact on a website, or changing a telephone number, although in reality dissuading a persistent attacker may not be so simple. Some young people are reluctant to block contacts from their phone or social networking site, as to not know what is being said about oneself can seemingly be worse than knowing.

Being out of the social loop is also a great fear for young people whose lives revolve around their connections with others.

Whether a victim of cyber bullying blocks the perpetrator's attacks or not, they may find they have little solace at home or outside of school, where a victim of physical or verbal bullying may be able to avoid attacks by avoiding areas where their perpetrators are known to be. But targets of cyber bullying will find it difficult to avoid attacks, what with computers in bedrooms and phones and gaming devices with Internet access can create an almost constant state of bullying from the original protagonist or others who join in the 'fun', particularly for young people who find it difficult to disconnect and whose existence revolves around their social connectivity. For those young people who find it difficult to create relationships and social connections in real life, the virtual world may be their solace and safety zone, where they can be anyone they wish to be. When this is threatened by cyber attacks, the conflict as to whether to disconnect or not is great.

Much has been cited about the '24/7' and repetitive nature of cyber bullying: once content is posted online or forwarded electronically it is virtually impossible for it to be retrieved or deleted – a sobering thought for young people whose whole lives have thus far been lived in the digital age and will continue to be as they apply for colleges and jobs in the future. The vast expanse of the Internet and the speed with which content can be copied, forwarded, downloaded and modified creates a permanence that most young people are completely oblivious to. As increasing numbers of employers and university admissions departments look online to learn more about their potential candidates, young people may find themselves missing out, thanks to unthinking actions in their youth.

While cyber bullying differs from more traditional forms of bullying, the results are still the same: fear, isolation, anger, panic and desperation leave many young people suffering in silence or seeking revenge.

Sexual, gender and homophobic bullying

Sexual, gender and homophobic bullying are not aspects of bullying that often receive much attention in education or awareness-raising campaigns. However, research suggests that they are a growing problem, closely linked to the wider issues of sexism, sexual harassment and abusive, unhealthy relationships among young people.

Sexist bullying can be defined as 'bullying based on sexist attitudes that when expressed demean, intimidate or harm another person because of their sex or gender' (Department for Children, Schools and Families 2009, p.5), whereas sexual bullying is defined as 'bullying behaviour that has a specific sexual dimension or a sexual dynamic which may be physical, verbal, or non-verbal/psychological'(ibid). Sexual bullying can take the form of innuendo or overtly sexual comments, offensive comments about a person's sexual reputation, and sexually offensive messages or written comments. A young woman's sexual behaviour can often be used as a target for relationally aggressive behaviour and bullying, even by members of her own friendship group. Rumours about a girl's sexuality, sexual activity or promiscuity can destroy her reputation, or girls may feel a pressure to engage in sexual behaviour before they are ready because of a pressure to fit in and be 'normal'.

These forms of bullying are particularly pertinent to working with girl relationship issues, as young women will often victimize other females using sexual insults such as 'slut' or 'whore', or spread rumours and gossip, and call other girls' reputations into question by suggesting a girl is engaging in sexual or promiscuous behaviour, or alternatively, questioning her experience with the opposite sex, such as suggesting someone is a virgin who cannot find a boyfriend. These sexually aggressive behaviours can be both subtle and overt and can ruin reputations and leave relationships in tatters. Girls engaging in sexual bullying may encourage boys to join in or communicate an acceptance of using sexualized language and insulting terms to women. Young men viewing women treating each other in this way can identify such behaviour as an appropriate and normal way to treat the opposite sex.

Sexual and sexist bullying disproportionately affects young women and girls, although boys and adults (including school staff) can also be targeted. The widespread use of sexual insults and the acceptance of women as highly sexualized beings from a young age, mirrored in the media, advertising, celebrity culture and commercialism, communicates a natural expectation that young women are to be desirable and desired, and viewed almost as a sexual commodity. Young women who act and dress provocatively, seeking to age themselves to gain male interest, often find themselves on the receiving end of unwanted attention from both men and women – whether as sexual attention, jealousy or bullying. The conflict as to whether to get male attention and potentially be targeted by other men and women as a 'slut', or avoid such attention and be categorized as a prude or frigid, can leave girls in a state of anxiety and confusion, and lead to poorly reasoned impulsive behaviours.

Homophobic bullying is closely linked to sexist and sexual bullying and falls on the continuum of gender and sexually related harassment. We define homophobic bullying as repeated or continual harassment that is both deliberate and targeted because of a person's sexuality or perceived sexuality. Young people and adults may be targeted homophobicly, whether they identify as lesbian, gay, bisexual or transgender (LGBT) or not, and many young women can find themselves on the receiving end of homophobia because of their non-conformity to traditional gender stereotypes or refusal to fit in with the 'norm', whatever it may be. The young woman who prefers to be friends with boys or who enjoys sports over shopping may find herself being labelled as a lesbian and viciously targeted as someone who is different and to be avoided.

The dynamic of girl friendship groups and the often desperate need for girls to feel as though they belong and fit in can lead to sexist, sexual and homophobic bullying. Until girls are supported to feel more confident and comfortable within themselves and to understand how to meet their needs for inclusion and belonging, this damaging behaviour will continue unchecked in our schools and communities. As girls become more socially and emotionally aware and learn to make more positive, self-affirming choices, their sexual and romantic relationships will likewise become healthier.

Chapter 4

The Complexity of Girls

Working with young women can be both extremely rewarding and incredibly challenging. As girls reach the end of primary school they have already begun a transition through periods of personal, social and physical growth. Childish ways are left behind and adulthood is yet to be reached, leaving teens in a 'middle ground' at a time of huge changes in academic expectation: primary school is left behind and so begins a period when friendships, interests and values are shifting. Suddenly girls are more aware of their physicality, sexuality and social status, creating a potential recipe for low self-esteem and confidence if girls are to navigate this crucial time unsupported.

As they reach early teenage years girls' awareness of themselves as a sexual being begins to grow, particularly through puberty. Often this occurs for girls before boys, who generally reach puberty later. As their physical body changes and sexuality develops, girls become increasingly self-conscious. The need for the safety of a friendship group becomes all the more crucial: friends are no longer simply playmates or those who share common interests, but a protection from being singled out and being seen to be different.

While girls become more physically and emotionally self-conscious during this period of adolescence, they largely still lack the maturity and self-awareness to be conscious of their inner needs and to know how to meet these needs resourcefully. A young woman may understand that she needs friends but may be unaware that the underlying need is for acceptance and inclusion at a time of personal upheaval and uncertainty in her body and mind. A young person who is unaware of what they need, and why, is likely to unconsciously meet her need through any means necessary, such as joining a bullying group of students for the safety of being in a group, even if it conflicts with her own values and her intrinsic needs for a more compassionate friendship. During puberty, girls' emotional needs will grow, many of which will go unmet as she struggles to understand why she is so suddenly needy and how she can feel more whole. Physical, hormonal and emotional changes can leave once-confident girls as shaky, uncertain teenagers. At this time girls will need greater levels of assurance, love, connection and comfort.

Girls with unmet needs for acceptance and attention, or even for love and support, will unconsciously seek to meet these needs in any way they can, such as trying to take centre stage in a social group by targeting another girl with bullying behaviour, gathering the group around her in support of her quest. Seeking to meet these intrinsic needs with destructive behaviour is unlikely to succeed for the long term, as is the effort of looking to others to meet individual needs; the group will never be able to consistently provide her with the support, love and acceptance she truly seeks. So begins a spiral of low self-esteem as the resultant negative outcomes and feelings eventually surface, such as the group rebuking her behaviour and isolating her, further exasperating her unmet needs.

All behaviours are tools and strategies to meet our needs, some of which are more positive and resourceful than others. Cooking a meal may meet a need for hunger, a need for creativity through our cooking, a need for nurture through the act of eating, a need for control over what we eat and how, or a need for approval and praise from our dinner guests. Each person's needs and how they are fulfilled is a completely unique and often unconscious process. The more aware of our needs we become, the more likely we are to be able to meet them ourselves rather than looking outside ourselves or seeking easy, quick or otherwise ultimately unhelpful methods of doing so. If a person has a passion for expressing themselves creatively, but this need is not met in their work or personal life, they may experience feelings of frustration, depression and lethargy, or just a sense that something is missing. The mature, self-aware person who is conscious of this need can track their negative feelings and current state of mind to the source of the problem – their unmet need for creativity – and explore ways to address this need and bring balance back into their life, perhaps by undertaking an art class, cooking a new recipe, or injecting more creative ideas into their work. This process of understanding our needs, acknowledging how they manifest as symptoms of unease if not met, and seeking ways to fulfil them creates a balanced, self-sufficient life. The child who feels the same urge for creative expression exhibiting as feelings of boredom and restlessness, but who cannot contextualize the feelings to be able to address them, may find themselves – perhaps almost unconsciously – engaging in extreme 'creative' behaviours that temporarily fill the need gap but ultimately cause greater pain and neediness, for example, displaying disruptive and aggressive behaviour in the classroom, drawing graffiti on public property, or flaunting school uniform rules in a bid for creative expression. Needs that escalate and run almost out of control, coupled with a lack of self-awareness, will only result in further low self-esteem as the desperate strategies used to try to meet these needs ultimately backfire, as depicted by Figure 4.1.

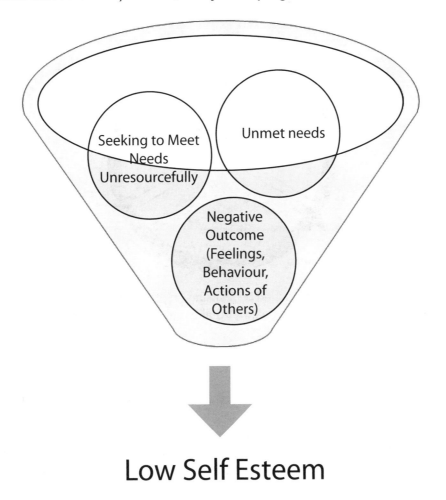

Low Self Esteem

Figure 4.1: The self-esteem spiral

Meeting needs in relationships

Relying on social relationships, particularly in adolescence, to meet key needs is likely to be doomed to failure, although this is a reality for many young women who are growing up in homes where there are few or no healthy adult attachments. A chaotic, inconsistent or abusive home is unlikely to meet children's physical, emotional and spiritual needs, leading young people to seek to meet these needs elsewhere. The young person who receives little attention at home, or solely negative attention, may display attention-seeking behaviours with friends or in the classroom. However, this is not to say that many of our non-essential needs can't be met through friendships and close relationships, such as our need for fun, relaxation and support.

If we can begin to build an awareness of what we need, we become empowered to know ourselves better and to know how to fulfil our basic and more complex requirements, including our emotional needs. We begin to acknowledge that we have the resources, tools and abilities to provide for ourselves most of what we need, including providing love, care, compassion and joy for ourselves. Once we acknowledge the vast amount of intrinsic inner qualities, we can look to others to complement us and 'top up' what we need. Love and kindness provided by another is much stronger when it complements the loving and kind actions, thoughts and beliefs we give unto ourselves. When we solely rely on another person or persons to provide all we need, our life becomes unbalanced and we deny our own inner resources, creating a sense of lack which further exasperates our needy state. A person who cannot show themselves compassion is unlikely to be able to fully accept compassionate words or deeds from another, nor be able to fully return that compassion.

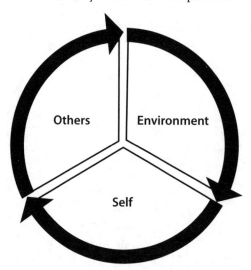

A balanced life is reached by focusing on others, ourselves and
our environment in healthy equilibrium to meet our needs.

Figure 4.2: The balance of life

A healthy balance between meeting our needs through our relationship with self, through our relationships with others, and through our relationship with our environment, ensures a balanced life between independence and interdependence and connection to one's surroundings, as demonstrated in Figure 4.2. However, an unbalanced life can create internal and external problems and conflicts, as Figure 4.3 denotes. The person who seeks to meet all their own needs and to be totally self-sufficient will undoubtedly become exhausted, isolated and resentful of having to do everything for themselves. A good example is the single mother who doesn't have any support or wants to prove her capability. Similarly, relying on our environment to meet all our needs, such as our work environment, may lead to burnout and a poor work–life balance. The student fixated on meeting their needs for approval, acceptance and accomplishment solely through their school work will not have a very rounded experience of learning and may lose their passion for studying and progressing on to further education. Meeting needs solely through relationships is also likely to be unsuccessful, as others withdraw from the weight of our neediness or we become resentful that others have their own needs and interests, aside from us.

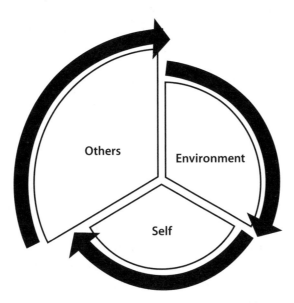

Unhealthy dependence on others to meet our needs leads to imbalances, conflicts in relationships, and a lack of focus on self and the world around us.

Figure 4.3: The unbalanced life

A key aspect of the Theme 1 activities 'Being Me' is to build girls' awareness of their inner needs and how those needs might be met on a daily basis *primarily by themselves, before looking to others*. Girls will explore their basic and non-basic needs and look for where those needs may be going unmet or where imbalances might be occurring, such as relying on a best friend to meet all their needs for fun, inclusion, support, friendship and so on. Exploring how to meet our own needs builds empowerment, resilience and self-esteem. If a girl can love and accept herself, feel at ease in her own company, and challenge herself to create meaning in her life, in addition to all those needs that will be fulfilled by others, she will have built a lifelong foundation of self-esteem, self-worth and resilience. Sadly, young people are rarely taught to acknowledge they have needs, never mind learning how to fulfil them. The activities in Theme 1 begin to build a foundation of awareness, helped by learning a vocabulary of needs-based communication to convey true feeling and to own thoughts, through the use of 'I' statements.

Thoughts – feelings – actions

Research and modern therapeutic theory tell us that our thoughts, feelings and actions are all interlinked, and how we behave is not solely randomized action, genetic or influenced by others. Our thoughts (including ingrained patterns of thinking) create feelings which may be extremely intense, particularly if the thoughts are often repeated and emphasized, thus becoming perceptions, which in turn cause us to behave in a certain way. For example, a colleague offers to help someone with a big presentation they have been asked to do by their boss. One person gratefully accepts, thinking that two heads are better than one and feeling a sense of relief that they now have someone to share ideas with. They respond enthusiastically, making plans to discuss the project straight away. For another person, the offer of help triggers ingrained thoughts of failure, not being good enough, and having to be rescued. These thoughts may escalate and grow in proportion until the person believes that the colleague was instructed to help as the boss believes she cannot cope alone. The whole office knows she is useless at presentations! These highly negative, downwardly spiralling thoughts create feelings of fear, self-repulsion, anger and mistrust. This person responds dejectedly, letting their co-worker take over, or perhaps responding hostilely, accusing them of not trusting their presentation abilities.

This theory of thought, feeling and behaviour is encompassed in cognitive behavioural techniques (CBT). The development of CBT is credited to renowned psychologists Albert Ellis and Aaron Beck, and is a combination of theories created to help people make changes in their life based on the premise of thoughts influencing feelings and behaviour, creating a consequence (Beck 1970). 'Faulty' thinking, or thoughts driven by strong feelings such as anger, will lead to inappropriate behaviour and the kind of consequences we often see in our schools. CBT is an increasingly popular form of therapy because of its research-based evidence, practical tools and rapid results. While CBT techniques are not generally used within the realm of the classroom, utilizing the main premise of CBT non-therapeutically to help build students' social and self-awareness can be highly effective.

The interplay of thoughts and feelings as drivers for our behaviour can help us to understand why people behave in the way that they do. Seemingly out of context outbursts and changes in character begin to make sense when viewed through the lens of being a consequence to some internal process. What we see is the end result of that process – the behaviour, actions and consequences. To fully understand what is going on for a person, or for a person to be in control of their behaviour, the thoughts and feelings drivers need to be examined.

Consider the young person who feels that a certain teacher 'has it in for me'. The student enters the classroom already filled with thoughts of injustice, unfairness, judgement and dozens of other perceptions formed over time and superimposed onto the teacher, until thinking of that person is synonymous with recollecting these furious thoughts. The more the student replays these thoughts, the stronger his feelings toward the teacher grow, as he becomes filled with anger, frustration and perhaps underlying hurt fuelled by unmet needs. In an already anxious and aroused state, the consequences unfold with almost textbook accuracy as a verbal altercation ensues, the student disengages from the classroom, and his thoughts about the teacher are confirmed. A similar process may be going on for the teacher who thinks that the student 'always wants to disrupt my lesson'. Helping the child – and teacher – to challenge and reframe their perceptions to create more empowering thoughts will dramatically alter their feelings, reducing the intensity of the emotion and therefore creating a different outcome. Helping each person to view the other as a real human being with their own needs, feelings and experiences can shift perceptions. The focus is on repairing and reframing the relationship to ultimately avoid conflict and bullying.

Utilizing the thoughts–feelings–behaviour model (Figure 4.4) to explore issues of girl bullying and relationship breakdown can be extremely useful, as girls have a higher tendency to ruminate about problems and create an ongoing internal process that feeds their emotional state. Girls may be more likely than boys to be aware of the subtle nuances of social interaction, creating a perception of the situation which may be inaccurate, depending on the level of emotional arousal and intensity of feeling. By exploring and challenging their thoughts, including their perceptions of others, students can begin to develop rational and reflective cognitive processes that challenge the appropriateness of the sort of behaviour they usually employ. This idea is reflected throughout the activities in Theme 1, where girls are challenged to identify patterns of thinking that lead to relationship breakdown. Girls are then empowered to make better choices, leading to better consequences for all.

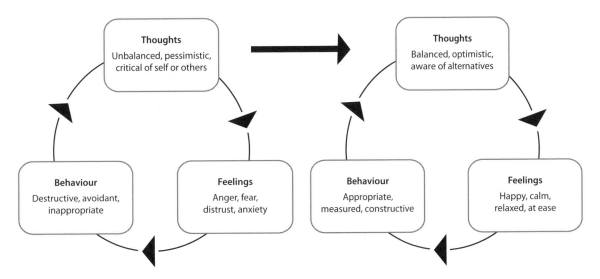

Figure 4.4: Thoughts, feelings, behaviours

I'm OK...aren't I?

If you are a teacher or other adult member of the school community, you will have undoubtedly taken on the role of counsellor, mentor, coach and shoulder to cry on for many students whose emotional distress and difficult life events obstruct their ability to learn. These days, awareness of mental health problems is far greater than ever before, although the stigma remains for many who feel subjugated by a society which categorizes mental and physical illness as two separate things, the former being less valid than the latter. This is also sadly true for millions of young people who find themselves taking anti-anxiety medication, battling an eating disorder or addiction, or defining themselves as depressed. Increasingly high numbers of young people are diagnosed each year with clinical depression, which paints a worrying picture for those young people who are yet to approach you for support, and whose desperate needs go quietly unmet.

Building a foundation of esteem, self-worth and resilience in children from a young age is absolutely critical, to arm them with the tools and self-knowledge to manage difficult life events in the future. Transactional Analysis (TA), created by Eric Berne in the 1950s, is a theory of personality and communication, exploring how people behave and interact in relation to one another. Berne's theories of relationships were publicized in the 1964 book *Games People Play*. A model from the theory of TA, the 'OK Corral' (Ernst 1971) explores how ingrained beliefs about the self can create a damaging and destructive perception of all aspects of life. The OK Corral defines four stances from which to view the world, as depicted in Figure 4.5.

The person predominantly inhabiting the first position of 'I'm OK; You're OK' has a belief that they are generally 'OK' and so is the rest of the world. This is an overarching perception that will of course have exceptions. Generally, this person has a strong sense of self-worth, and believes others to be worthy and good in nature, too. This young woman would likely be able to form and maintain strong and trusting friendships and avoid relationally aggressive techniques to deal with conflicts. In a bullying scenario, this girl would shrug off nasty comments made about her, knowing them not to be true, or seek support to talk through her feelings of hurt. She would not 'own' those comments about herself as fact, as she generally believes herself to be a good, worthy person. This girl is also more likely to forgive her persecutor or provide an empathic explanation for their behaviour, such as acknowledging the attacker has a poor home life. This girl would be least likely to be targeted by bullying or relational aggression as typically she is well supported and has a strong social circle.

I'm OK; You're OK	I'm OK; You're not OK
Secure attachments High self-esteem High sociability Trusting and accepting of others Positive self-image Optimistic outlook	Anxious attachments Fearful, angry, boastful Exaggerated self-image Inability to relate to others Low trust in others 'Dangerous world' and defensive mentality Higher sociability
I'm not OK; You're OK	**I'm not OK; You're not OK**
Dismissive attachments Low self-esteem Low confidence Low sociability Poor self-image Need for inclusion and acceptance Victim mentality Negative self-perception; exaggerated positive perception of others	Fearful attachments Low self-esteem Low sociability Victim–persecutor mentality (cycles of being both) Negative perception of self and world Pessimistic outlook

Figure 4.5: The OK Corral

The next position – 'I'm OK; You're not OK' – is that of the person who feels that they are worthy, but others are not. This person may feel others are out to get him or that he lives in a dangerous world. He may also feel that he is better than everyone else, and will look down from a position of superiority, leading to an inability to form authentic, trusting relationships. A young woman inhabiting this position may play the role of 'Queen Bee', elevating her own social status in the group and showing little empathy or compassion for others. The girl who believes the world at large to be 'not OK' may display negatively proactive behaviours, 'getting in there first' by spreading a rumour before someone can spread one about her.

The third position – 'I'm not OK; You're OK' – is that of the person with low self-worth who elevates the status of those around her. She may have a poor self-image and a victim mentality, believing that she is a worthy recipient of aggressive and abusive behaviour because others are better than her. A classic example of this is the woman who continually finds herself with a cycle of abusive partners. In a girl bullying scenario, this child will most likely be the pervasive passive and submissive victim who is persistently targeted by others. She reports being bullied but constantly returns to the friendship group, only for the same thing to happen again, as if on repeat. This girl may also make fun of herself to get the attention and acceptance of the group, downplaying her achievements and abilities and up-playing the attributes of others. Her low self-esteem keeps her locked in a position of inferiority.

Finally, the fourth position – 'I'm not OK; You're not OK' – describes that of the person who believes neither themselves nor others to be worthy. This highly negative and pessimistic outlook may create cycles of playing the role of victim, followed by persecutor, an example of which being the child who is perpetually a victim of bullying and simultaneously identified as a protagonist for such behaviour by other children. What might be termed as a 'provocative victim' this child will just as likely report bullying as cause it. The provocative victim, a term coined by bullying researcher Dan Olweus, describes the child who appears to be seeking out instances to be victimized, perhaps by displaying overtly odd, irritating or hyperactive behaviours that draw negative attention (Olweus 1973, 1978). The provocative victim often exasperates staff who struggle to know how to encourage the child to avoid people who react aggressively to him or situations that perpetuate the bullying problem. However inappropriate the behaviour, this child may be completely unaware of why they do what they do and feel locked in this victimized position because of their 'I'm not OK' thought position.

Martin Seligman (2007), the groundbreaking pioneer of the field of positive psychology, researches and writes of the importance of an optimistic outlook and a positive sense of self. Having hope, viewing events and situations through a positive lens, and generally having an optimistic reasoning style – that is, how we explain the world to ourselves – creates greater happiness, better relationships and better health. With any child involved in a bullying situation or embroiled in relationship dramas and relational aggression, a tendency to ruminate, dwell on negativity and create a generally negative perception of life is a danger that ought to be avoided. Whether victim or bully, rumour-spreader or receiver, how a child explains the event to themselves, processes what is happening, and draws conclusions will create patterns of thinking, and ultimately, beliefs. Children who regularly inhabit the roles of 'I'm not OK' or 'You're not OK' are in danger of accepting these self-loathing, fear-inducing positions for life. A pessimistic attitude and outlook is not born with children; rather, it is developed over time, largely by accepting the models of thinking of key adults who create huge impressions on small minds. The good news is that it can be unlearned, particularly by using techniques such as CBT, which helps people become aware of and learn new patterns of thinking.

Consider whether any young people you know match the 'OK Corral' descriptions above, and whether their underlying emotional needs are being met. The potential for problems in later life is great for those inhabiting the three 'not OK' roles, and just as likely to surface in the classroom or school life now. The girl group 'leader' who rules through manipulation and creates dramas to rival any soap opera storyline may well be acting from a position of 'I'm OK; You're not OK', just as the girl who strives to fit in at any cost may view herself and others in terms of 'I'm not OK; You're OK'. Having an awareness of these roles and their impact can inform your classroom practice and day-to-day interactions with young people, as well as assisting them to build more positive perceptions of themselves and others through character education and programmes such as *Surviving Girlhood*. By exploring the roles of the OK Corral we can begin to understand why some people behave in the way that they do and become aware of what their underlying needs may be. Many of the subtle characteristics of these roles will have been modelled by key adults or impressed upon children through the words and actions of caregivers and other adult role models, such as the child who is consistently told they are stupid and dumb eventually inhabiting the mental position of 'I'm not OK; You're OK'. Programmes and curriculum that build children's self-esteem and self-awareness and that promote the importance of choosing how we think, feel, and act in response to situations will help children break free of limiting self-beliefs to move to a position of empowerment, self-assuredness and confidence.

As Figure 4.6 denotes, how we relate to ourselves influences how we relate to and connect with others, which in turn influences how we connect and relate on a wider level with our community and society. Individuals who do not have respect for themselves and do not value their own contribution will unlikely be able to truly value friendships and connections. This in turn denotes how the individual views relationships (they are used as a tool to gain power or popularity, or for personal gain, as opposed to a means for connection, support, care, love and so on). Poor social connections and a lack of value placed on cultivating strong and supportive relationships with others will undoubtedly be demonstrated in a lack of respect for school property, an uncaring attitude about the wider community, a lack of connection to others and the surrounding world, and a general sense of apathy. This may also explain why some children become passive bystanders or even collude with bullying behaviour: their lack of concern and inability to feel compelled to take action may speak of their own lack of self-value and appreciation.

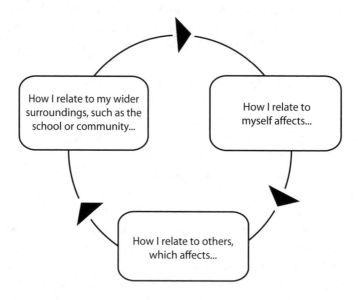

Figure 4.6: The cycle of influence

The drama triangle

Young women living the pessimistic roles created by the negative perceptions of themselves and the world around them may find themselves caught up in cycles of drama and crisis in their personal life and relationships, fuelled by the surrounding media and celebrity dramas and peers playing similar roles.

Parents and teachers will be well versed with the cycles of drama that keep some girls riding the highs and lows of school days. For some young women there is little awareness of a relationship *without* drama, which is likely to follow girls through to their romantic connections and parenting as behaviours become accepted and learned as the norm, such as having to make one's partner jealous to confirm their romantic feelings. Drama-filled relationships, whether friendships, romantic pairings or parenting relationships, will leave participants locked in a dance of extremes – stress, anxiety and conflict following perceived closeness, romance or comfort, only to be followed by the low extremes once again as the next wave of drama erupts and breaks the tenuous calm. As girls build beliefs that relationships are supposed to be filled with drama, little room is left for healthy, supportive relationships or people who don't submit to the idea of love or friendship being synonymous with behaviours like backstabbing, arguing, threats and emotional outbursts. Teen television programmes, films and music that portray relationships in an overly dramatic sense also present young people with an inaccurate perception of what it means to connect with others; the 'soap opera effect' creates a distorted view of human interaction that can appear normal if repeated or witnessed enough, even if only through television.

Stephen Karpman developed a model of drama in the 1970s which can help us to understand the interplay of relationships and roles with which young women can engage. The drama triangle

(Karpman 1968) depicts three distinct roles – the victim, rescuer and perpetrator, as described in Figure 4.7. A person can inhabit one role, such as that of a victim, or can shift roles, such as from victim to perpetrator to victim in an ongoing cycle. The triangle demonstrates the relationship of roles – the victim needs a perpetrator to perpetuate the role, as much as the rescuer needs a victim to save. Playing a role can provide the person with a sense of identity and confirm their place in the world. Even though the role is overtly negative, such as that of the victim, there is a sense of safety in knowing one's place in the world, and perhaps even a reward in the status of the role. Albeit an unconscious process (as mostly the person playing the role is unaware that they are doing so, so ingrained the beliefs and learned behaviours have become) the role may meet a person's need for attention or support. Shining a light onto alternative, more resourceful ways to meet their needs will help young people break free of these roles and live a more authentic, fulfilled life.

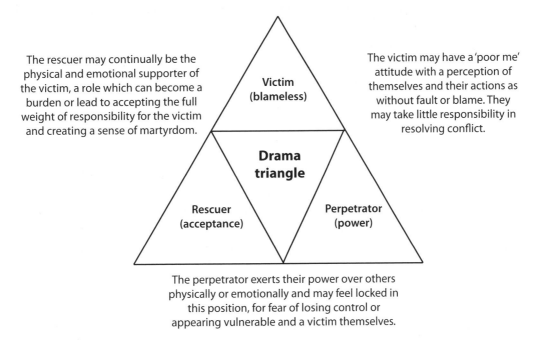

The rescuer may continually be the physical and emotional supporter of the victim, a role which can become a burden or lead to accepting the full weight of responsibility for the victim and creating a sense of martyrdom.

The victim may have a 'poor me' attitude with a perception of themselves and their actions as without fault or blame. They may take little responsibility in resolving conflict.

Victim (blameless)

Drama triangle

Rescuer (acceptance)

Perpetrator (power)

The perpetrator exerts their power over others physically or emotionally and may feel locked in this position, for fear of losing control or appearing vulnerable and a victim themselves.

The roles are fluid and can be interchangeable. A victim can become a perpetrator, and vice versa. In a friendship group, an instigator of bullying can lead other girls to play the role of rescuer, or to become protagonists against the bully, resulting in her then becoming the victim, and so on.

Figure 4.7: The drama triangle

The language that girls use can be a key to identifying the roles they may be playing, and thereby helping them to move beyond the drama cycle. A young woman who is caught in the role of a victim may use language such as 'I can't', 'They made me', 'It's not my fault', 'I'm not good at…' and so forth. The role of the victim in particular is important to explore with young women, as it can also be a powerful position, albeit a highly negative one, for the girl who gains the support and attention of her peers or adults with her victimized behaviour. This girl may find that being a 'poor me' can prompt others into action as they rush to her side to offer words of comfort. In this sense there may not even need to be a real persecutor for the young woman to play victim – consider the girl who comes into school looking downcast and teary-eyed, alluding to something terrible her parents or boyfriend may have done to her. The interesting tactic of making up stories or rumours about oneself describes this position of the powerful victim, such as telling her friends that she has an eating disorder or that her boyfriend hit her. The frisson of excitement that is felt by being so close to such dramas can create a tighter bond between friends, despite compounding a highly negative self-perception and set of behaviours for the perpetual victim as she starts to own this perception and experiences the negative consequences that follow, such as friends eventually challenging the validity of her stories and withdrawing their support.

It is important to note that many people inhabit these roles unconsciously and are often not aware of the language they are using, techniques they are employing, and the way they are engaging with others in the push-and-pull of the drama cycle. A young person may have learned to create a victim mentality by modelling the behaviour and attitude of her mother, or the aggressive techniques for asserting power over others from her father or other key adults. It is also important to stress that for these young people, constantly moving around the drama triangle and inhabiting these roles may be the best way they know how to meet their needs. Developing their awareness and exploring alternative behaviours and attitudes to meet needs more resourcefully can help girls break free of this almost constant cycle, thus avoiding the potential for drama-infused relationships and parenting in later life. Regardless of whether this role playing is a conscious behaviour or not, girls need to be challenged to accept responsibility for their thoughts, feelings and actions and to choose more resourceful alternatives. Adults who excuse, explain away, dismiss or pity poor behaviour without action are doing children a disservice, as they will never learn to break free of these negative positions.

As young people begin to learn more about themselves at a deeper level of understanding and build awareness of their thoughts, feelings, values and beliefs, they become better equipped to make individual choices to affect larger processes, including friendship group dynamics and bullying cultures. The young woman who is developing an awareness of what it is to be a true friend will begin to reflect on her behaviour and choose not to spread rumours and gossip. The girl who explores how the media influences her may choose not to buy into the idea of 'thin is in'. The student who is exploring how she meets her needs for inclusion and acceptance may develop more appropriate ways to feel a part of something. These individual processes create a chain of reaction that spreads positive peer pressure and role models throughout the school and community.

Identity

As girls are beginning to understand themselves better, the topic of identity is introduced within the theme of 'Being Me'. Our identity characterizes how we see and describe ourselves and what we identify with. Exploring our identity can help us define who we are and to redefine who we want to be. Challenging our young women to explore their perception of who they are promotes the idea of making a conscious choice about our personality, characteristics, cultural beliefs and what we identify with. By exploring what their identity is, girls develop awareness of how their identity was formed, including through external influences such as the media.

Adolescence is a time when individuals begin to find their voice and start to enact a sense of free will. It is at this time we see young girls begin to act in ways to win their peers' approval, even if this behaviour is likely to incite the disapproval of their parents and other adults. When working with girls it is important that adults understand what drives their behaviour if we are to address the issues they present on a daily basis. All too often, however, young girls embroiled in friendship disputes are labelled by adults, who fail to give the time necessary to explore the underlying issues, and whose responses are likely to be 'This is typical of you'. Encouraging young girls to explore their identity and understand their needs, values and beliefs, which form our sense of self, will provide them with an opportunity to understand themselves better. Girls can then learn to trust their choices and inner voice, which in turn will develop healthy development and trust in others.

In his theory on personality first published in 1950, Erik Erickson (1995) argued that every individual progresses through eight stages of development throughout their lifetime, and at each stage an individual will unquestionably go through a crisis which they must experience if they are to progress onto the next stage of their development. Adolescence is acknowledged as the critical period for identity formation and development of the self and it is during this time that individuals experience conflict between the development of their own sense of self and the emerging influence from their peer relationships. For young women this is a particularly crucial stage of development as they struggle to form their sense of self while navigating their way through often unhealthy friendships and the bombardment of conflicting messages from the media, peers, parents and teachers.

The influence of modern technology also has a critical impact upon the development of identity at this time; young people are increasingly using their assumed anonymity on the Internet to form different identities and personalities and to adopt different roles with their so-called online 'friends'. This can have a detrimental impact upon a young girl's development and will often have a negative effect upon their sense of self; developing different personas, especially if they conflict with a person's values and beliefs, can lead to pain, confusion, anger and frustration, which is either internalized as the young person becomes depressed or aggressive, or externalized through risk-taking behaviours. It can often be frustrating for adults when responding to friendship disputes, especially as young girls will be reluctant to leave their friendship circle and form more positive and healthy bonds with others, but as Erikson (1968, p.130) points out, adolescents will identify themselves 'with the heroes of cliques and crowds to the point of an apparently complete loss of individuality'. Exploring the reasons for forming often unhealthy relationships with others through encouraging young girls to examine what identity is and what it means to them can engender a healthier outlook on friendships and conflicts.

Boundaries

Our personal boundaries define what we are comfortable with and how we expect others to treat us, including how we expect to be spoken to, challenged, touched, treated in a friendship or romantic relationship, and what we are willing to do in our work, social interactions and life in general. Our boundaries are rarely spoken of but are always communicated through our actions or our interactions with others, and even in our body language. The person with very loose personal boundaries may unconsciously expect to encounter aggressive behaviour from their partner, or may feel that sexual willingness is a prerequisite for having a boyfriend, or that having multiple romantic partners at once is appropriate. In a school setting, a lack of boundaries may result in students being repeatedly victimized, becoming the target of bullying and isolation, as they do little to communicate (verbally or non-verbally with their actions, facial expressions or body language) their disapproval or rejection of what is being done to them, giving their tormentor the green light to continue.

Putting personal boundaries in place is not something often discussed in schools but is crucially important, for both staff and students. Exploring boundaries helps girls to identify the behaviours they are and are not comfortable with and understand how they are communicating their expectations. A young woman who does not want a boy to touch her romantically or sexually without her permission will need to have personal boundaries in place to communicate this. Often this communication is subtle and without words. Problems occur when girls' expectations of their boundaries conflict with the messages they are communicating, such as not wanting to be touched by a member of the opposite sex but wearing provocative and highly sexualized clothing, perhaps because of media and societal pressures to follow fashions. This is not to say that a woman's dress, nor any other actions or choices she makes, constitutes a right for another person to abuse, dominate or intimidate her. It is, however, an important learning point for adults to impart to young people about the importance of how their actions, words, dress, demeanour and so forth send messages to others.

Chapter 5

Influences

In today's technologically advanced, multimedia world we are constantly bombarded with information that seeks to educate, inform, persuade and inspire us, ultimately grabbing our interest and influencing our thoughts, feelings and desires, one way or another. A study conducted by market research firm Yankelovich Incorporated found that we view over 5,000 advertisements each day, all of which are trying to influence the way we live our lives and spend our money.

Avoiding these many influences is hard and often nonsensical – TV programmes, advertisements, magazine articles, books, our friends, our family and our wider culture all help to shape our desires, beliefs and values. From early childhood we are influenced by those around us, and from these influences we create our sense of self. This is a natural and generally positive process when our influences are largely healthy, appropriate and positive. However, as many parents and educators are discovering, the surge of influences inundating young people can often be destructive, negative and inappropriate, despite the perceived normality of these pressures by young people and society in general. Theme 2 'Influences' of *Surviving Girlhood* explores the various external influences young people may face, helping girls to discern how they are positively and negatively influenced by the world around them and how to consciously choose to avoid unwanted pressures.

Many of us can feel the pressure of the fast paced world, with constant contact via phones and email and the need to maintain social connections through social networking sites. Adults who grew up in a pre-Internet world can probably remember a time when making a phone call required being next to a phone, and sending a letter was a good way to get in touch. Our children and young people, born into the digital age, have always inhabited this electronic world and are potentially more au fait with a life revolved around technology and media influences. They quickly grasp the changes in technology as it advances, often leaving behind parents and adults in their knowledge and understanding of technology. But as we note the incidents of bullying, aggression and relationship breakdown in our homes and schools, perhaps we are inclined to be concerned about how these influences are affecting our young people. The ineffectuality and impossibility of trying to shelter young people from the modern world leads us to consider how character education (such as social and emotional learning or curriculum that seeks to build students' sense of identity, self-esteem, leadership and so on) can grow social and self-awareness to better equip young people to identify and discern external influences. Children and teens who are more aware of their internal needs, values and feelings can better comprehend their place in the world and make more informed choices about how and by what they want to be influenced and how their actions will influence others.

Influences, beliefs and values

Cara is 14 years old, well liked, and generally a good student. Cara's career goal is to become a glamour model. The TV programmes she watches show Cara that drama, arguments and mistrust in relationships are normal, and celebrity is key. The magazines she reads subtly and overtly inform her that she needs to look prettier, be thinner and wear the latest fashions, whatever they may be. She adds contacts to her social networking profile whether she knows the people in real life or not, because having more contacts indicates popularity. She communicates with her friends constantly via text messaging and thinks nothing of spreading gossip or rumours because all of her friends do this too.

Cara's values and beliefs are an example of those held by many young women today, whose lives revolve around social connectivity, the world of advertising, celebrity and pop culture. While clearly the majority of women and girls can read a fashion magazine without developing an eating disorder, the impact of external influences cannot be underestimated as we consider how external influences become internalized views and lifelong beliefs. These beliefs can create a negative self-perception, low self-esteem and confidence, anxiety, depression and a lack of self-worth, all of which are expressed in destructive, damaging behaviours.

Our beliefs are largely formed in early childhood, as we acknowledge and process the beliefs of key adults around us as our own. Our beliefs provide us with 'benchmarks' about the world around us, helping us to make sense of, and contextualize, people, places and things. Growing up in an overtly racist household can create the same beliefs about race in children, who claim these beliefs as their own, for example. For many children, as maturity develops and influences by peers and other key adults can be discerned, beliefs are reviewed, altered or discarded. Typically, we are drawn to others who share our key beliefs and values, whose attitudes and lifestyles complement our own. If young people fail to discern their values and beliefs as positive or negative and discard those that are not self-supporting and resourceful, they will inevitably befriend peers and find role models who reinforce their negative viewpoints, values and beliefs. Problems occur when negative influences become internalized as our own thoughts and beliefs, creating a cycle of influence within ourselves through our words and actions and becoming our own force of negative influence to others. These beliefs then set forth a chain of motion that dictates what we value as most important to us. A belief that self-worth is contingent on having certain physical attributes to be accepted by peers will lead a person to value themselves only when they feel they are looking good, are dressed in the right way, or receiving the right attention from friends or the opposite sex – an unfulfilling and inconsistent way to meet their needs for acceptance and acknowledgement.

For some young people, underlying low self-esteem and self-worth can create a susceptibility to external influences, while for others, prolonged or intense negative influence, such as associating with a deviant peer group, can create the same resultant outcomes. Regardless, it is clear that there is a need for our young people to become aware of the influences around them, understand their effects, and feel empowered to choose with whom and what to associate.

Blindly accepting the opinions, supposed 'facts', attitudes and information of others (including family, peers and the media) can create problems that are all too real in our schools and communities, and bullying is no exception. How many teachers have seen first-hand the generalized acceptance of bullying, passed off as being 'part of our culture' – for example, 'If he hits you, hit him back!' Racist, homophobic, sexist or generally aggressive and judgemental attitudes create the behaviours we want to eradicate from our schools and communities. Educating and inspiring young people to develop critical thinking skills to discern for themselves the validity of the influences around them will create a lifelong ability to maintain a strong sense of self.

The susceptibility of girls to external influences

Many TV shows, films, magazines, games and commercials are aimed primarily at adolescents, who represent huge consumer power. At this age, young people are more vulnerable to being externally influenced and are likely to be attracted by illusionary, immature and faulty thinking, represented by celebrity culture, advertising and peers. The social nature of girls and the importance that young women place on their relationships with others can create a higher susceptibility of young women to external influences, all due to the key adolescent need of fitting in with peers.

Young women account for a huge percentage of fashion, beauty and technology sales and many teen girls have a profile on social networking sites such as Facebook. As society dictates how young women should dress, where they should shop, what music they should listen to and what food they should eat, the pressure increases to meet their need for acceptance, approval and inclusion within a social dynamic. Young women who are bisexual or lesbian, or who are questioning their sexual identity, may struggle with external influences to an even greater degree, as young gay people are so inaccurately and under-represented by the media and in common society.

The security and status provided by the social group is key for young women: the need to fit in will encourage many girls to be negatively influenced by their peers and conform to the group's expectations, to the detriment of their own needs, values and beliefs. Many young women will eventually accept the group's values as their own, leaving parents exasperated and confused as to why their little girl has suddenly started dressing, acting or speaking in a completely different way.

Media influences: The sexualization of young people

The portrayal of both men and women as sex objects can be readily seen almost everywhere, with models and stars portrayed in a sexual manner, wearing revealing clothing and displaying a look or manner that implies sexual readiness. This has helped to create a generation of overly sexual young people, who convey a look or manner of physical maturity but often lack the emotional awareness, resilience and confidence to cope with the after-effects of sexualization. Young people are surrounded by sexualized images, advertising and a general suggestion that one must appear sexually attractive to the opposite sex. The dramatic shift in the content of music videos, for instance, clearly demonstrates the huge emphasis on sexually open and provocative behaviour indicating attractiveness and desirability.

Sexualization is defined by the American Psychological Association (2010) as occurring when a person's value comes only from her or his sexual appeal or behaviour, to the exclusion of other characteristics, and when a person is portrayed purely as a sex object. The sexualization of young women can lead to a lack of confidence, depression, eating disorders and a negative effect on healthy sexual development, in addition to skewing the perception of boys and young men of how members of the opposite sex should be treated and what it means to be in a romantic relationship. Premature sexualization influenced by magazines, advertising and the media generally can lead girls to feel a pressure to look older and dress in a more adult way. The desire to fit in, be accepted by a peer group and avoid isolation can lead young women to give in to these pressures to act and behave in a sexual manner. Many friendship issues within girl groups, particularly with older girls, relate to boys. The rumours of who did what with whom, boyfriend stealing, and general in-fighting as to who is more desirable to the opposite sex can destroy friendship groups and lead to sexual bullying.

Sexualization can also create self-objectification, whereby a young woman learns to think and treat her own body as an object of desire, defining her own needs and state of being as synonymous with that of young men's, for instance, choosing what to wear in terms of what she thinks will be most attractive to men; allowing boys to engage in sexual acts with her whether she wants to or not; or taking her boyfriend's opinions, likes and dislikes as her own, losing her own sense of identity. She learns to treat herself as an object to be viewed, judging her value on her appearance and how desired she is by the feedback she gets from members of the opposite sex, even if this feedback is crude and inappropriate. This inevitably leads to low self-esteem and a lack of self-worth and self-respect. Self-objectification has also been linked to poor sexual health and reduced sexual assertiveness in young women, as their inhibitions, values and sense of judgement are usurped in favour of being desirable and desired, ultimately to meet underlying needs of acceptance, approval and love.

The media and self-image

From a young age children are subjected to gender ideals and messages that dictate what it is to be a boy or girl, as obvious as children's clothing often being pink or blue. Boys are given messages like 'don't cry', while girls are unconsciously encouraged to take the role of mother and housemaid with toys such as dolls, prams and kitchen sets. Coupled with the influence of the media, young people are increasingly subjected to the promotion of gender stereotypes and a pressure to conform to a gender ideal – looking thin and overly sexual for women and appearing masculine and muscular for men.

Stereotypes can be a helpful way to understand and quantify the world, but can lead to a limited experience of life whereby one conforms to an imposed ideal. This may be particularly difficult for those who do not or refuse to conform to generalized ideals, for example, young lesbian, gay, bisexual or transgender (LGBT) people, who may find themselves stigmatized or reluctant to live as their authentic self for fear of prejudice, bullying and abuse.

The common gender stereotypes for women (appearing submissive, emotional and vulnerable) and for men (being the breadwinner and head of the household) are slowly being usurped for the next generation by the celebrity ideal, assisted by the onset of reality TV programmes. The promotion and infamy of glamour models, singers, actors and the 'highly paid and badly behaved' sports stars is creating a new gender ideal that is just as limiting for young men and women as previous stereotypes. The media and celebrity stars increasingly portray women to be glamorous, desirable, sexual and unintelligent, while men are presented as 'bad boys' and emotionally distant. The apparent approval by society of provocative dress, cosmetic surgery, aggressive and outlandish behaviour, binge drinking, and a range of other negative and destructive actions modelled by the celebrity world are creating spirals of damage and chaos for young people who have yet to build a sense of self and clarify who they are. The next generation is increasingly accepting these behaviours as normal, indicating that they are acceptable activities to replicate.

Young people's exposure to gender stereotypes needs to be balanced with education and awareness-raising of the alternatives to conforming to a stereotypical view and the importance of creating and maintaining their own sense of identity and self-image. Girls can be shown alternatives to the stereotypes filling their TV screens and magazines, and encouraged to explore who they are in relation to these stereotypes, deciding whether they are positive or negative influences for them. This exploration develops critical thinking skills that help young people discern for themselves how they want to behave and who, if anyone, they want to emulate. Media and gender stereotypes are explored in Theme 2 activities.

The media and behaviour

While sex and violence seem to have become the accepted norm on TV, in music, films and popular culture as a whole, the impact of viewing such behaviour cannot be escaped. US researchers found that young people who watched the most TV shows with sexual content were two to three times more likely to become pregnant or to impregnate someone than were teens who watched the least, while young people who most frequently visited websites depicting real people fighting, shooting or killing one another were five times more likely to report engaging in violent behaviour than were those who never visited violent websites (Anderson *et al.* 2008).

As teens take more social cues from the media than ever before, it is not surprising that schools find themselves dealing with aggressive, bullying and violent behaviour on a regular basis as scenes from popular TV programmes influence their behaviour and young people view such behaviour as normal. Groups of children gathered around a bullying incident to chant their support is an indication of the desensitization to violence and young people's acceptability and perceived normality of such behaviour, while the increasing tendency to film and post such incidents to the Internet communicates an even more worrying trend – that violence is not only normal, but also something to be shared for pleasure and enjoyment.

Young women may have learned a host of inappropriate, manipulative, relationally aggressive and abusive behaviours from films and TV programmes that suggest that drama, deceit and power struggles are par for the course in a romantic relationship or friendship. The mean girl persona of the popular girl who 'rules the roost' by dominating and manipulating others to follow her lead and do her bidding creates an atmosphere and culture of pervasive bullying and conflict, leading to an overall school climate of fear and inequality. Likewise, skewed attitudes and beliefs of how to romantically relate to another person can lead to dating violence and domestic abuse, such as believing that arguing and constantly splitting up and getting back together is a normal part of a relationship.

Using technology to influence others

The role of the media in influencing our thoughts, feelings, beliefs and values is clear: increased susceptibility or prolonged exposure to pervasive negative attitudes in various forms of the media (and from key peers and adults) can create an unhealthy mind-set, behaviours and values. What is also apparent is the role of media and technology to influence others, such as using the Internet to gain support and backing to humiliate someone. The growing problem of cyber bullying, where technology is used as a means to hurt, degrade and harass, is a prime example of how technology can be used as a method of manipulation, to spread rumours and gossip, to exert power over another, shift social dynamics (such as isolating peers by engaging in online discussions they are not privy to) and ultimately bully and intimidate others.

The impact of cyber bullying and associated behaviours is explored in Theme 3, 'Respect, Responsibilities, Relationships'.

Family influences

Young girls' experiences in modern western society differ dramatically from their experiences over a hundred years ago. The expectations of girls to achieve academically and aspire to fulfil successful careers, in addition to continuing to fulfil the traditional female roles, such as caring for the family, places significant pressures on women to achieve balance in their lives. Nowadays, young girls witness the stress, anxiety, guilt and pressures placed on their mothers to succeed in all aspects of their lives, from caring and providing for the family, to progressing in their career. Many women will convey their guilt at leaving their children to go to work and often face criticism if they strive to be successful in their career. It is rare for a mother to get the work–life–family balance right so that they experience a well-balanced lifestyle. This is observed by their adolescent daughters, who are in the process of forming their own identities and are looking to their parents, in particular their mothers, for guidance at this time.

Expectations for young girls to achieve in all aspects of their life – socially, personally and academically – can have a detrimental impact upon their development of self and can leave many girls struggling to form their own identity. Individuals very often take on different personas and act according to the social circle they find themselves in; a young woman may act politely and respectfully in front of her parents and strangers, but may swear and behave brashly in front of close friends. Girls will often act in accordance with the social convention; they may play the dutiful daughter with their parents and be the vivacious teen in front of their peers, drinking and acting in promiscuous ways to be accepted and fit in. This can be difficult for girls who are in the process of discovering their real self. Acting differently in different social circles, often hiding their true self to ensure they are accepted, leaves them confused and questioning their values and beliefs. Brown and Gilligan (1992) suggest that girls experience a relational impasse in adolescence, where they struggle to understand their identity and often hide their real self, preferring to act in ways that conflict with their beliefs and values rather than fall victim to the humiliation and verbal assault that occurs during adolescence when one goes against the social grain. As discussed earlier, during adolescence, as girls are in the process of forming their identity, their own sense of self becomes suppressed in preference for maintaining unhealthy peer relationships.

Parents can often be guilty of forcing girls to maintain these unhealthy relationships. Where parents influence a girl's friendships and encourage their daughters to form friendship bonds with children from their own social circle, it can be difficult for girls to move away from these friendships for fear of upsetting their parents or inciting their parents' disapproval. These friendships are typically cultivated from a very young age and are reinforced through social gatherings and shared activities, such as joining daughters in the same clubs. Cultivating friendships in this way can lead to relational aggression as girls grow up and begin to discover the basis of their friendship was based entirely on their parents' friendship and they have very little or no shared interests, values or beliefs. It becomes difficult for young people to navigate the friendship from the point where they discover their relationship goes no deeper than the bonds of their parents' friendship.

When parents cultivate friendships, they often push their daughters into friendships that can be unhealthy, causing them to question their identity, misinterpret their values and beliefs, and behave in ways that may cause harm to their social, emotional and academic development. Take, for example, the young girls whose parents are close friends and sporting enthusiasts. One daughter finds herself enjoying watching and playing sport, which is encouraged by her parents and her friend's parents. The other child has no interest in sport, and instead enjoys playing instruments and writing her own music. This child will undoubtedly find herself joining sporting teams for the approval of her parents and to share an interest with her friend, despite these activities having no appeal. Her lack of interest may lead her to put little effort into the team games, causing arguments with her friend and parents. Ensuring that she continues to be liked and accepted by her friend and to prevent arguments means partaking in activities that hold little or no interest for her and suppressing her own values and beliefs. This in turn causes internal and external conflict with the child, who will find herself continually begrudging her friend and finding fault in her performance, behaviour and attitudes. Girls who find themselves in similar situations often discover they are in continuous arguments with their friends as they find more faults in their actions. When a young girl is unable to recognize that she is partaking in activities that are detrimental to her values and beliefs, which in turn is detrimental to her self-development, her inability to achieve in this area and the internal conflict she is experiencing because she is not living in alignment with her beliefs and values, inevitably gets projected outwards.

Parents influence their daughters' relationships with others in many ways, far more than they would with their sons, such as becoming embroiled in their daughters' arguments with their friends. It appears to be generally accepted by parents, indeed by society, that when boys fall out they will fight and move on from the argument, and this is true in many cases. Unlike boys, a girl will hold on to something that was said or done towards her by another individual for a long time and can recount these words and actions months after the encounter took place. Parents are likely to fuel these arguments too. If their daughter comes home from school stating that the other girls were being unkind and explains her version of events to her parents, they can become very defensive. In many cases, parents will complain to the school expressing their anger and frustration at the lack of support and action taken to protect their daughter from such behaviour. Increasingly we are witnessing parents directing this anger at the alleged 'perpetrators' through the use of social networking sites and, in some cases, face-to-face confrontation. This will undoubtedly exacerbate the problem and cause further friction among the friendship group.

It is not only arguments with their daughter's friends that can exacerbate problems for a young girl. Arguments between parents can directly impact upon their children and the fall out of such arguments can be witnessed in schools and in the community. Young girls, as with boys, feel pressured into continuing their parents' 'fight'. Professionals working alongside girls express their frustration and anxieties about addressing problems presented to them by young people whose parents are caught up in an ongoing cycle of conflict. They question how they can address issues presented by the girls in schools and youth settings when the problem actually stems from parents and the issues in the wider community. Such behaviours presented by parents have a negative influence on their child's behaviour and relationships with others. How can children learn to effectively communicate with others when their dominant role models find it difficult to effectively and appropriately respond to conflict and maintain healthy relationships?

Psychologists have long argued that phobias and other behaviours are learned through observation and reinforcement from positive and influential role models. Children are quick to pick up on their parents' anxieties and worries and in the majority of cases will start to own that behaviour as their own. If a mother demonstrates a fear of spiders in front of her toddler child, the child observing this behaviour will begin to process this information and interpret the actions as a significant way to behave when spiders are present. In the same way parents unconsciously pass on both their ambitions and their insecurities to their children, which can influence a child's decisions when it comes to selecting friendships, interests and career choices.

Girls whose parents are well educated and value the importance of academic achievement, career or a vocation will likely be encouraged to achieve academically and supported in their choices to attend university and move away from the family area if this will benefit future career choices. Parents with little or no formal education and whose perception of schooling is highly negative may be less likely to encourage academic development and advancement in education. It can also be said that some girls are actively encouraged to drop out of school and have children at a young age. When mothers are supportive of young girls becoming pregnant and leaving school as soon as formal education ends, it can be difficult for those professionals (who see potential in these young girls to be successful in their education) to break through the influence of their parents and encourage them to remain in education and go onto achieve higher qualifications. A young woman at this period in her life can often find herself being submissive and playing roles to meet the standards placed upon her by the significant people in her life. To this end she finds it difficult to find herself and establish an identity that is true to her own values and beliefs. Conforming to a set of standards placed upon her by others often leads to a young girl being in conflict with herself, which in turn directly affects the relationships she finds herself in, both platonic and romantic.

What Dana Jack (1993) termed 'silencing of the self' can often be seen among girls who maintain these sort of relationships, keeping their true selves suppressed in order to maintain harmony among the group. Many young women fear rejection by their peers, in particular their friendship groups, if they voice opinions, dress in their own unique style, or simply enjoy certain activities or academic subjects. The encouragement of such friendships can have a detrimental impact upon a young girl; it prevents them from developing successfully through the adolescent stage of their lives and often leads to depression, isolation and guilt. When we explore with young girls what qualities of their friends are important to them, their answers always reflect loyalty, personality, trustworthiness and honesty. Maintaining relationships based on social advancement and being accepted by their peers, rather than interest, personality and trust, can cause internal and external conflict for young girls, and those traits most important for friendships to flourish are often missing. It appears that young girls know what traits they value in their relationship but often are unable to transfer this into reality, where their relationships with others in their friendship groups often lack the traits they want, and indeed need, from their friends in order to develop healthily through the adolescent stage of their lives.

Anxieties felt by parents about their daughters' friendships, experiences at school and social interactions often pass onto the child. A parent whose first words to a child as she walks through the door from school are 'What did they do to you today?' is inviting the child to reflect on the negative interactions she had during the day, which can often over-exaggerate a disagreement with friends or a comment made by another student. The words parents use as their daughter returns from school are important and can help a young girl build self-esteem, confidence and resilience. Martin Seligman (2007), in his writings about optimism, highlights how parents whose best intentions are to support their child and bolster their self-esteem and be encouraging can actually have the adverse effect. Often parents who think that they are building self-esteem by telling their child everything will work out for the best, next time it will be better, or try to do activities and take control of situations for them, can cause a child more harm because their thought process becomes clouded with negativity about their own ability to achieve and resolve problems. Parents need to encourage reflective thinking and problem solving in their child while at the same time acknowledging and validating the child's feelings. Parents should impart information that allows children to realize that failure and negative emotions are only temporary and changeable, and not pervasive and permanent, as some young people often view friendship disputes and conflict (Seligman 2007). Pervasive and permanent thinking can cause further problems in a girl's relationships within her friendship group, as her thinking becomes clouded with judgements about herself and how others view her. Any comments made or actions that she considers are directed to put her down in some way will serve only to reinforce her negativity about herself. This in turn can be internalized, presenting as depression or other forms of mental health problems, or externalized through arguments or physical harm to others.

An adolescent girl faces many challenges during these years, and it is important that parents encourage the development of an emotionally intelligent and empathic daughter who is able to resolve conflicts in effective and positive ways. Berndt (1982) stated that conflict resolution may be as important as cooperation in friendships, and girls must be aware when they are experiencing conflict and know how to respond to it effectively when it occurs (Nadeau 1992). Often girls will not recognize when they are in conflict with their peers, and as such, could find themselves in situations they did not want to be in, particularly when the issue of boys and sex comes into play. What may initially begin as banter and a bit of fun talking about boys or sex, with her friends, can quickly turn into a situation that a girl had not meant to find herself in, such as being drunk at a party and being encouraged by her friends to kiss a boy she has liked for some time, or worse, being encouraged to partake in sexualized behaviour. This behaviour is often internally justified by girls if it means being accepted by her peer group, but more often, it leads to negative consequences such as rumours, gossip and relational conflict.

Parents play an important role in nurturing and encouraging girls to explore options that will enable them to develop self-respect and autonomy. Learning to respect one's self is an important element in achieving healthy well-being and stability in relationships. Self-respect will inevitably lead to girls being comfortable with the person they are and will develop their confidence, which in turn will ensure that girls are able to make the right choices in life and not feel pressured to partake in activities, or indeed find themselves in situations that put them at risk of being in conflict internally and externally, within their friendship group. Young people find it difficult to be autonomous and stand up to their peers to do the right thing, but it is important to encourage this in young people if we are to fuel change and develop both individuals and a society that are caring, respectful towards others, and emotionally and socially responsible. Parents' failure to encourage young women to develop self-respect and autonomy, and their encouragement of friendships based on social circles rather than interest, personality and trust, can lead to girls being at the centre of disagreements between friends and even the creation of cliques and bullying. This, in turn, leads to a community of distrust, selfishness and an inability to show compassion to themself and the world around them.

Socialization has an important role to play in a child's development, and parents' values and beliefs are often adopted by a child without question. As such, a child may develop attitudes that conflict with the values of society, their peers and their school. This can lead to internal and external conflicts for the child who is trying to establish their own unique identity and find a place in friendship groups and the world. For girls in particular, this can be difficult as they try to maintain relationships with their mother and friends, while developing their own sense of self. If a mother places an importance on sporting activities, such as team games, and encourages the development of friendships based on these values, it can affect a daughter whose interests may be more in solitary activities, such as playing a musical instrument. This can also be said of parents who hold strong prejudices and beliefs about others, which are often transferred unconsciously to children who present these in their interactions with their peers. This can have a detrimental impact in schools and communities where there is a rich diversity of cultures and beliefs, and can lead to continuous conflicts between peers. Parents can often promote pursuits and friendships that fit with their values, rather than encouraging their daughter to explore different activities and interests in an attempt to discover their own identity. This may feel more comfortable for parents, whose primary aim is to keep their children safe and protect them from harm, knowing the world as they see it through their own eyes and potentially distrusting anything that may be different. Parents who do allow girls to explore alternative activities and interests often do so with strict boundaries in place, for example, allowing children to explore interests only within the confines of their religion or ethnicity. This in turn can cause internal and external conflict for a young girl who may question her parents' choice of religion, and want to explore her own choices and expand her knowledge and understanding of the world and its people and strive to discover her true self through discovery, trial and interaction with others.

Cultural and peer influences

Our culture plays an important role in defining our attitudes and beliefs, and it can be difficult to determine one's true identity when bombarded with images of women who are thin, rich and idolized by others (particularly if they are idolized by males), broadcasting the message that young girls must look, behave and think in a certain way if they are to be accepted by their peers and society. Girls are constantly subjected to subliminal messages that convey that society's acceptance of a person hinges on being in a romantic relationship; images through the media, literature and popular culture all portray women who are only looking out for one thing, going after and getting 'Prince Charming'. This is often reinforced by girls' mothers, particularly if a mother behaves in a way that suggests her self-esteem is linked to being in a relationship. Some girls observe their mothers moving from one relationship to the next, which can be tumultuous and destructive, leaving young women feeling as though they need the support of a male partner to feel any self-worth. Fathers also impart their values and beliefs onto a daughter's relationship, particularly if they encourage the belief that no man will be good enough for their 'little princess'. This thinking encourages some girls to have unnaturally high expectations, not only in her romantic relationships, but also in her friendships.

Mikel Lyn Brown (2003) argues that girls are taught from a young age that other women cannot be trusted and that they are constantly 'out to get their man' and destroy their reputation, which only exacerbates tensions between females. Indeed, when you identify the main cause for most girls' fights, arguments and gossip, boys often play centre stage as the topic by which to humiliate a girl or are used to increase tensions already existing in friendship groups. Having a boyfriend increases a girl's status within her friendship group and can be played to her advantage, but she can quickly find herself with a lot of enemies if the romantic relationship suddenly ends. Girls who impart information about boys they have a 'crush' on to the person they trust most, their 'best' friend, often find that their so-called friend has told other girls, or worse, told the boy in question. This kind of behaviour can be even more destructive if girls impart information about any sexual activity with boys.

With the advancement of technology, the cause for concern with many girls is so-called 'sexting', a form of communication used by many young women to please their boyfriends, but one which has unfathomable consequences for the sender of such messages. What may begin as innocently sending a few provocative pictures to a trusted partner can quickly become an action that many young girls regret. These pictures are often circulated to other peers in the school or community, causing humiliation, rejection and hatred from her friends to the point of a student becoming isolated from her peers or even refusing to leave her home for fear of reprisal. In some cases this is taken further as the pictures are posted online, where there is no hope of the student getting control over who has access to her image. The detrimental impact this has upon a young girl's emotional and social well-being must not be underestimated, as the consequences of this perceived innocent action can remain with her for the rest of her life. Professionals and parents alike need to understand the reasons why young girls feel the need to partake in such activities, which are often the result of low self-esteem, self-worth and unmet underlying needs.

Just as the media can influence young people, society and a young person's cultural background can also influence their thoughts, beliefs, values and behaviour. Young girls from ethnic minority backgrounds can find it particularly difficult to develop their sense of self through adolescence, and friendship groups are often narrower as a result. External experiences such as racial discrimination and differing religious and family values can make it difficult to fit in to defined social groups that do not match cultural upbringing. Differences in values and beliefs can also make it difficult for girls to form positive friendship bonds with girls from different cultures and religious background without some sort of internal or external conflict taking place. Some will experience this conflict from within their own ethnicity, particularly if they question any part of the values or beliefs of a given culture. Trusting friends from different backgrounds can feel risky when girls experience racism or prejudice in their communities and society as a whole. They may question the attitudes and values of their friends, which can cause tensions in relationships and lead to a high number of conflicts.

As girls grow older, their friendship activities become more centred on boys. Standing around the playground watching boys play sports or dressing in a certain way to gain a boy's attention can be normal behaviour for girls but can also be difficult for some young women whose religious and cultural values place strict rules or expectations on interactions with the opposite sex. When it comes to socializing or partaking in conversations about boys, it can be awkward and uncomfortable for girls to join in when their values clash with those of their friends. The interactions with boys can have severe consequences for some girls, not only among peers but also with family members. Take Farah, a 15-year-old girl who has been struggling to maintain a firm friendship group. She has floated from one group to the next, leaving in her wake a number of conflicts with different girls in her year group. Farah's father has boundaries that he expects her to adhere to, and most importantly he values academic success and encourages Farah to do well in her studies, ensuring she spends time after school finishing homework and studying for tests. Farah has found it difficult to maintain friendships as she struggles to preserve the perfect daughter facade and simultaneously to play a friendship role and fit in with others. Her friends are always talking about boys and are constantly encouraging Farah to tell them who she likes. In an effort to maintain the status quo, Farah began to tell her friend that she had been in a relationship with a certain boy and that she had 'done stuff' with him. This culminated in rumours being spread around the school that Farah was pregnant.

Sexual bullying of this nature is not uncommon among girls, many of whom feel the pressure to have sexual intercourse or to experiment in sexual activity before they feel comfortable to do so, simply to appease friendships and to fit in, only to experience an onslaught of name-calling, abuse, threats and exclusion following these experiences from girls once viewed as friends. It can be difficult to tell parents about the problems a girl is experiencing for fear of them believing that she may have partaken in such activities and receiving disapproval about the nature of the bullying. The unwillingness, or inability, to inform her parents or other trusted adults about the problems she is experiencing can lead to a young girl internalizing her problems, and potentially to depression and maladaptive behaviours such as self-harm, alcohol abuse and drug misuse. It is important that girls are aware that they can talk to their parents or other trusted adults about the problems they are experiencing and will not be judged, or worse, be made to feel that they were responsible for the problems occurring in the first place.

Peer pressure can have a major impact upon girls' behaviour and actions, leading a young person to undertake activities that she does not feel comfortable with, such as excluding others, name-calling, ruining reputations or engaging in sexual activity, just to fit in or to avoid being the next target. Girls look to their friends and peer group for cues on how to behave and respond to situations. If there is a culture of backstabbing, gossip and put-downs, it is likely that girls will behave in the same way in an effort to fit in. During adolescence, it can be very difficult for any young person to stand out from their peers and avoid being drawn into the drama that unfolds during the school day or on social networking sites. Young girls especially feel compelled to be involved in the social interactions of their peer groups, even if these can be negative and draw girls into a series of ongoing arguments, friendship disputes and peer rejection.

An individual's behaviour is often influenced by the group they are part of. Homophily, the tendency for individuals to befriend others like them, is common among girls who behave in accordance to the subjective norms set by the group. Failure to conform to the unspoken rules and norms of the group, such as not wearing clothes from high-end retailers or refusing to drink alcohol at parties, could lead to isolation and to personal and social attacks from others. Girls will admit to witnessing acts of bullying behaviours perpetrated against one individual and will also admit to doing very little or nothing at all to prevent it. They cite their fear of being the next target as the reason for failing to intervene and to stop the onslaught of abuse directed at one individual. Girls believe that to defend another individual or to speak out against the subjective norms of their peer group could lead to the group turning on them. When an environment does not provide support, understanding or skills to individuals to enable them make a stand against negative behaviours, it can be difficult to stand up to those who subject others to humiliation and emotional and social harm.

Young women witness negative behaviours on a daily basis, and adults will often dismiss this as the route to establishing friendships and a part of young people forming peer groups and growing up. However, girls realize it is much more than just a part of forming social connections, especially when the intention is to hurt another individual. This belief from adults and the inactivity from other peers make it difficult for children who witness negative behaviours, know it is wrong and want to do something to help. When they look around for cues from their peers and teachers and notice they are ignoring it, joining in or laughing along with it, they do not feel confident that they will be supported if they do something to help.

Status is a key element to relational aggression, and often those girls who are popular among their peers can be the cruellest, such is the sway they hold with their peers to support their negative actions. This can be very difficult for adults to believe, as these are often the individuals who are willing to help out without being asked, do well academically and portray prosocial behaviour in the presence of adults. However, other girls are often subjected to the manipulation and hurtful gossip that is circulated in an effort to destroy reputations. This behaviour can be escalated by other members of the peer group, and the popularity of individuals often strengthens as a result. Girls, and even some boys, welcome being part of and accepted by the social group and will undoubtedly join in and act negatively towards other individuals.

Pushing boundaries

Young people will push the boundaries of acceptable behaviour and expect to be challenged if they overstep these boundaries into unacceptable action. A part of growing up is to test and push the confines of rules which aim to establish a sense of responsibility and awareness in young people of what is acceptable in society and what is not. Testing boundaries has long been a way for individuals to understand societal rules, and when challenged, individuals learn right from wrong and are encouraged to take responsibility for their actions. When left unchallenged, young people cite their contempt at others for failing to confront them; they lose respect for adults and authority figures if their behaviour is condoned.

Failure to challenge young people when they push the limits of respect or break the rules implicitly gives the message that it is acceptable to behave in this way and dilutes the boundaries and rules set by society. For example, it was once socially unacceptable for young people to drink alcohol or smoke, and if they did, it would be out of sight of adults, knowing that they would be punished and receive reprimands from potentially any witnessing adult, not just their parents. However, in recent years it has been more prominent for young people to drink alcohol on the streets, often in front of adults, and to smoke on school grounds, even if this is out of sight of teachers. Our failure to challenge young people over their actions, often fuelled by reports of youth annoyance in the media, has in essence given them permission to behave in this way. Indeed, many adults will cite fear of attack when they see a group of teenagers and will cross the road to avoid any contact. This portrayal of young people has two consequences: first, it takes power away from adults and reinforces to young people that they can behave in uncivilised ways in their communities without fear of reprisals. Second, failure to challenge unacceptable behaviour prevents a learning opportunity for young people, and as adults we fail to raise a generation of responsible citizens.

Young people also look to their peers for cues on how to act, and if peers support their actions they will continue to behave negatively towards others. Peers are extremely influential in promoting or preventing bullying behaviours; Craig and Pepler (1997) noted in their research, 'Observations of bullying and victimization in the school yard', that bullying behaviours stop in less than 10 seconds in 60 per cent of all bullying incidents when peers intervened.

Therefore, peer influences can also promote positive behaviour if nurtured and encouraged. Harnessing the influence that peers have in escalating or preventing bullying behaviours is key for our schools and communities. Providing young people with the skills they require to positively challenge negative behaviours when they are presented is essential to promote caring, respectful environments that nurture positive relationships.

Chapter 6

Understanding Relationships

It can often be difficult for young girls to navigate their way through the minefield of friendships and come out on the other side feeling confident and compassionate. As highlighted in previous chapters, our culture is experiencing an escalation of what has been termed 'girl bullying', but there is often a reluctance to identify and respond to this behaviour. This may well be because, as adults, it can be difficult to define what is actually occurring in girls' friendships as bullying or conflict. Adults often mistakenly categorize the grievances faced by many girls as a normal part of growing up, establishing friendships and overcoming minor disputes. As such, individuals who are caught in the eye of the storm are often given little time by adults to uncover what is occurring during these apparent friendship disputes and are all too often told to wait it out until it is over. However, ignoring the problem, or failing to identify what is actually occurring within friendships groups, can have devastating and long-lasting consequences for those caught up in the drama of girl cliques. This applies to all individuals who are caught up in the drama cycle and not just the young girl who appears to be the 'target of the month'.

Managing relationships at a young age can be very difficult for a girl who finds she is struggling to fit in with the social expectations of her friendship group. It is wrong to assume that young women will know how to respond effectively to difficult situations and that they will make the right decisions when faced with dilemmas that challenge their values and beliefs. The prefrontal cortex part of the brain is the part that helps us rationalize, make decisions and moderate correct social behaviour. The functions carried out by the prefrontal cortex area relate to abilities to differentiate among conflicting thoughts, determine good and bad, determine future consequences of current activities, work toward a defined goal and predict outcomes. The prefrontal cortex isn't fully formed in young people until around age 20. Therefore it is no surprise that children when asked will say 'I don't know why I did it' or find it difficult to see the consequences of actions, such as bullying. This is not to say that children's actions should be dismissed because their brain isn't fully developed, but we do need to teach them to nurture these skills. Every child needs to be taught how to manage conflict effectively and, just as importantly, how to manage relationships. As explored earlier, young girls are presented with images and messages from the media, parents, adults and peers that can all reinforce negative relationships with other girls. Mikel Lyn Brown (2003) argues that images of backstabbing, gossip, rumour spreading and other women trying to destroy romantic relationships are in abundance in our culture. It is for this very reason that girls need positive reinforcement and positive role models to turn to as a means of readjusting the scales and it is important that significant adults are able to provide them with such role models.

Self-respect

Adults often talk about respect but at times fail to express what this means in terms of the individual and their interactions with others. An increasingly high percentage of girls in our modern world have a poor sense of self-respect, and many more lack an understanding of what self-respect means to them. Adults talk about raising self-esteem and confidence, but to ensure that a young woman achieves social, emotional and academic equilibrium, a sense of self-respect also needs to be achieved, indicating an acceptance of ourselves for who we are and liking all aspects of our physical, moral and spiritual being. Raising the self-esteem of children and young people has increasingly become a task of schools and educators; the so-called 'self-esteem movement' of the 1970s and 1980s fizzled out after test scores didn't seem to correlate with increased positive self-perception. More recent research and attempts to place social and emotional learning, and with that increased self-esteem, back onto schools' agendas will surely help young people feel better about themselves in the short term, but what happens when they are faced with adversity and again begin to evaluate themselves based on their current situation?

Raising self-esteem so that children and young people create a healthy self-concept must be combined with developing self-respect, so that increased self-esteem can be actionable. Without self-respect during times of adversity, it can be difficult for girls to remain centred and on-course rather than channelling their negativity into destructive behaviours. Adults place a great emphasis on raising a child's self-esteem to ensure they perform better, their well-being improves, and they are more emotionally and socially adept, but they ignore the fundamental need that every individual has: the need to accept oneself for the person we are. Feeling good about oneself, acknowledging our attributes and talents, and holding positive beliefs about our character are all crucial to healthy self-development. Respecting oneself encourages us to put these aspects of esteem into practice, by making the right choices, choosing positive actions, and generally living in alignment to our beliefs.

Often, as professionals and well-meaning adults we strive to develop children's self-esteem, praising children, focusing on external achievements and trying to 'build them up'. While this is an important role, and perhaps not one fulfilled elsewhere in some children's lives, failure to understand and address what is driving low self-esteem in the first instance will not create healthy self-concepts, and crucially, self-respect.

Figure 6.1 demonstrates the push-and-pull of raising an individual's self-esteem and neglecting to work on establishing a positive and healthy sense of self: if we concentrate on building self-esteem alone, we will find ourselves in this constant cycle of resolving relationship problems as they arise, with girls stuck in a continuous cycle. After adult intervention it appears that the problem has resolved itself, but it is not long before a girl is referred for further work or support because she has been drawn back into the friendship drama cycle. Encouraging children to build their own self-esteem, and developing their understanding and implementation of self-respect, will create a far stronger basis for future well-being and will create resilience. Parents, teachers, counsellors and other professionals agree that resilient children will be better able to cope with adversity and life's challenges.

Resilience helps children to manage the conflicts they face in their peer groups and navigate their way through the drama cycles that often present themselves in girls' friendships. By working with girls to accept themselves and to adopt a sense of self which is positive and accepting of their abilities, personality and appearance, they become resilient individuals who can respond positively to rumours, gossip and negative comments. Young girls who are confident and respect themselves will be able to make positive judgements in line with their sense of self and the reality of what is opinion or fact. Being able to make these judgements enables girls to weigh their options in positive and healthy ways and not respond negatively when confronted by behaviours that aim to attack their reputation or demean their sense of self.

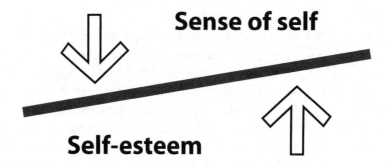

Figure 6.1: The push-and-pull of self-esteem and sense of self

It follows that without self-respect, no individual can respect others, as they will undoubtedly find the faults they see in themselves in those who surround them, pushing the negativity they feel towards themselves onto others. It can be difficult to see that we earn respect through our actions rather than command true respect of others; young people, indeed even some adults, often mistake fear as respect. A person who follows the commands of someone with a reputation for being aggressive and intimidating does not do so obligingly but rather out of fear of the consequences if they do not. True respect is given to those individuals who show compassion, understanding and interest in those around them and expect nothing back in return. True respect can be earned only if individuals have confidence in their own abilities and have respect for themselves. They will be unable to show the compassion or selflessness required to obtain true respect from others if they do not respect themselves. Instead, respect is demanded, often due to the need to gain extrinsic rewards from others, such as status, power and a feeling of worth.

Without self-respect we are unable to show compassion and understanding towards others because we constantly project outwards our own insecurities and flaws. This leads to behaving in a manner that can be construed as bullying, such as gossiping and using jokes and name-calling to put others down, often as a means of making the perpetrator feel better about their own faults. This behaviour can have an adverse effect on an individual, who in the first instance may feel satisfaction at lashing out at those flaws they do not admire in themselves, but satisfaction turns quickly into feelings of guilt and shame for hurting another person and for behaving in a way which conflicts with their own values. This in turn perpetuates the insecurities a person feels and reinforces the negative thoughts they hold about themselves, moving further away from self-respect.

Responsibility

Human rights laws are designed to ensure every individual has a life with their basic needs for survival fulfilled. Earlier we discussed the needs we all have as humans for safety, food and acceptance and the detrimental impact on an individual of not having these needs met. It is true we all have the right to live free from humiliation, harassment and victimization, and young people are very quick to point out if their rights are being abused or ignored by others. Indeed, many adults will say that young people have too many rights and as such this has led to a generation of young people who are disrespectful and antisocial. This behaviour, however, is not the fault of young people knowing their rights, but rather the misguidance of adults who teach about rights but fail to pass on an understanding of the responsibilities that young people have as active citizens within their community and the world at large. Indeed, when a young person behaves in a manner that causes pain to others (which may also mean emotional and social pain), we often do not provide opportunities for them to take responsibility for those actions and learn from their mistakes. As adults, we take the responsibility away from young people by doling out punishments and sanctions for behaviour, or ignoring their actions and leaving them unchallenged. This is not to say that sanctions are not required when a person has caused harm, but sanctions alone do not encourage young people to take ownership of their actions and to accept responsibility for the harm they have caused.

Some young people will even go as far as stating they welcome expulsion from school; in many cases young people will view expulsion as a positive means of escaping an institution they do not feel comfortable being a part of, often having been labelled by adults as a troublemaker. On their return nothing has changed or been learned, no amends have been made, and the child is further estranged from the learning process and the idea of school as a positive place, where they can learn skills that will set them on the right path in life to become active and positive adults. It is important that we teach young people that they have a responsibility to ensure they treat others with respect and have the right to be free from harassment and victimization themselves.

Young people have a responsibility to themselves as well as others; this responsibility to ourselves is often overshadowed by the responsibility we have towards others. Few people will take the time to actually listen to their own body and thoughts and take responsibility for them, and all too often we expect others to take responsibility for us, whether for our actions or to direct our course through life. All too often we use the phrases 'But they did' or 'It's all his fault'; when we think about friends who discuss their relationships with their partners, how many of them take responsibility or mention their role in an argument? It can be difficult for girls to see where responsibility for their actions and behaviours lie. Girls often cite their friendship group as the reason they began to partake in certain activities, such as gossip, name-calling, put-downs or, more seriously, drug-taking and sexually promiscuous behaviours. When girls interpret events, actions and situations in their lives by looking toward external forces to explain their actions, such as parents, teachers or peers, they deny their own involvement and responsibility and blame these external forces for their own thoughts, feelings and behaviours. In other words, 'It is the fault of others that I feel so bad'. Adults fail to teach young people to reflect on their own input into situations and their own role in the behaviours they portray. In some cases adults actively encourage girls to play the role of victim and allow them to continue to blame others for the situation they find themselves in; by punishing the perceived perpetrator the adult implicitly reinforces the thoughts of the child: 'See it was their fault', 'Why else would they be punished?' Teaching young people to take responsibility for their actions in given situations will build their capacity to continually reflect on their thoughts, feelings and behaviours and learn to adopt solutions to their problems and identify more positive means of responding to situations.

However, this is not to say that young people experiencing bullying and pervasive conflict should be made to feel responsible for the situation they find themselves in. Many victims of bullying will naturally feel that they must have done something to incite such hatred and meanness from others; a young person in this situation should be supported to understand they did not cause the bullying, but they do have a choice as to how to respond, including telling someone, accessing help and support or choosing to take positive actions, such as removing bullying contacts from a social networking site.

It is essential that we teach girls to take responsibility for themselves; failure to do so will often lead them into unhealthy relationships, both romantic and platonic. Young girls have a responsibility for their social, emotional and mental development and often need guidance on how to understand their thoughts and emotions. Adolescence is a difficult time for any individual, but for girls it's a time of hormonal changes, confusion and upheaval, combined with the added pressure of fulfilling the traditional and modern-day female role. Trying to be all things to all people can be challenging for girls, many of whom are expected to start having romantic relationships during adolescence, achieve academic success and maintain relationships with peers, despite these relationships being all too often destructive to their well-being. It is during adolescence that many girls start to partake in promiscuous behaviours, often fuelled by peer pressure or a lack of self-respect and self-esteem. Teaching young people to manage romantic relationships is becoming more commonplace in social-emotional and character education programmes, but managing relationships with friends is still overlooked, despite the growing awareness of the problems experienced by young girls in their friendship groups. Focusing on respect and responsibility for ourselves and for others assists us in teaching girls to manage their relationships within friendship groups. Knowing their responsibilities will help to foster a sense of self-respect, which in turn will flourish a respect for others.

Relationships

Managing relationships in the modern world can be difficult for anyone, particularly young women. Mihály Csikszentmihályi argues:

> We are biologically programmed to find other human beings the most important objects in the world. Because they can make life either very interesting and fulfilling or utterly miserable, how we manage relationships with them makes an enormous difference to our happiness. (Csikszentmihályi 2002, p.164)

The changing face of friendships as a result of modern interactive technologies has made it even more difficult for girls to fit into, understand and manage the dynamics of their friendship groups. Friendships vary from virtual to real-world friends, and girls need to learn to manage the dynamics of both. There often appears to be an expectation among young women that they must be friends with everyone and, if not everyone, at the very least the right people. This often means fitting into social norms that conform to the popular girls in school but which may conflict with their own sense of self. As girls move into adulthood, however, their friendship groups become smaller and the drama that would once take place in their schoolday friendships becomes less frequent, if not entirely eradicated. However, women, as well as girls, will often find themselves in conflict with friends if they have grown through life partaking in behaviours that have never been challenged; they will continue to gossip, put others down and manipulate friendships to get what they want, as behaviours become ingrained and entrenched. Young girls witness this behaviour in their mothers, family members and other significant adults, which in turn reinforces the behaviour they portray in their friendships in school and the community. Young girls need guidance during the years they begin to form friendships to prevent problems emerging.

Pre-adolescence is increasingly becoming the period of time when girls begin to experience problems in their friendships with others. Gossip begins to spread around school, girls float from one friend to another, and manipulation begins within peer groups. Working alongside girls who are experiencing problems with their friendships provides us with insights into where relationships begin to break down. Young girls become preoccupied with avoiding becoming the next target rather than looking out for and providing support to their fellow peers. Relationships become very fragile because of this, as girls start to analyse every statement, action and situation. For many girls, friendships become fluid as they move from one peer group to the next to avoid being the target of rumours, put-downs and exclusion. The basis of friendships is built on lies and misconceptions as girls try to avoid verbalizing their feelings or acting in ways that may upset someone else in the group. An unspoken set of rules transpire within friendship groups, which, if broken, can lead to destructive consequences for the individual who broke them. This can be very challenging for a new girl at school who is unaware of the social expectations or for those girls who fail to keep up with any changes in the rules, such as knowing the right clothes to be worn or the 'correct' means for communicating in text messages and online.

Friendship can be a difficult concept to grasp for any young girl. You are expected to have friends and enjoy the company of others, and as Mihály Csikszentmihályi (2002) points out, it is innate in us humans to seek out other humans. We cannot deny the biological need to be in the company of others; the human species has evolved to adapt to a life where we require cooperation to survive. Women have always required the social and emotional support of other women to help raise children and learn to provide a caring, loving environment for their family. So why then, if we as humans require social contact with others, do we experience so many problems in our relationships? The concept of friendship is one that we are all familiar with: someone who cares for you, looks out for you, is there when you need them, and someone to share common interests and activities with. It is our hope that our main relationships with our friends are exactly of this type and we are able to enjoy the company of our friends without drama or ill feeling. Friendships tend to go wrong or start to experience problems when we fail to communicate our thoughts and begin to interpret events, actions and words in ways they were not meant. This is particularly true for young girls who are still in the stage of their life where they are trying to establish their own sense of self. Perceptions of the self are often skewed in adolescence; just as hormonal changes start to take place an individual begins to learn more about the world around them, and confusion sets in as they begin to discover the world from a different perspective to the one provided by their immediate family. It is difficult for a child to accept opinions and facts that contradict those provided by their parents: trying to establish their identity and their place in the world comes at a time when adolescents are subjected to academic pressures, which adds to the stress and confusion that all young people experience at this stage in their life. As we discussed earlier, the pressure felt by individuals to conform to the norms of their peers is great at this time and failure to do so often leads to being ostracized, humiliated and victimized by their peers. This is a lot for young people to manage, especially when there is little or no guidance on how they should deal with their thoughts and feelings. The impact this in turn has on relationships is demonstrated by the number of conflicts experienced by young people on a daily basis, many of which are not reported or witnessed by adults. Education policy has recently attempted to address this issue through the promotion of well-being in schools and the introduction of social and emotional learning.

Communicating with friends, while experiencing such confusion, becomes very difficult. Young girls are not always aware of their own sense of self and often adopt the values, opinions and beliefs of the friendship group. At times when girls find themselves at odds with the opinions and beliefs of the friendship group, it can be difficult to communicate this to others. This is often because they fear they may be ostracized by the group, but it also comes from a lack of awareness of themselves and the reasons why they feel so at odds with others, and so are unable to communicate effectively their thoughts and feelings when issues arise. Teaching students that they do not always have to agree with their friends to remain on good terms and that there are appropriate ways to communicate differences without causing disputes and relational conflict can assist in promoting the well-being of the individual and reduce the number of friendship issues faced by young girls.

Managing conflict

Usually adults become aware of issues experienced by girls only when the problems have escalated to cause significant emotional and social harm or when physical attacks have occurred. It is often at this stage in friendship arguments that professionals are called upon to resolve the issue. When talking to those involved in the disputes, we hear that the arguments, gossip, name-calling and other behaviours often stemmed from a minor misunderstanding or an argument which was not resolved in an appropriate, respectful and effective manner because our young people were not taught how to resolve conflict in appropriate and positive ways. If adults think back to their own childhood, it is unlikely they will be able to identify when they were taught to resolve conflict; instead this is often something that we observe and capture from role models in our lives. Learning to resolve conflict by observing parents, teachers, peers and other influential individuals in a young person's life can, and often will, result in negative and ineffective conflict resolutions being adopted if the role model's behaviour is flawed.

As educators and professionals we need to understand the importance of teaching young people to resolve conflict from an early age, as children as young as three years old will adopt distinct ways of resolving conflict by acting aggressively, such as snatching toys, or using passive responses, such as ignoring the problem and moving on to another task to avoid conflict. However we choose to respond to conflict, resolution will either have a positive or negative outcome, and it takes a lot of skill to determine how best to respond in any given circumstance. For example, take the person who cut you off while driving; you may choose to confront this situation by flashing your lights, following the person, screaming at them and using hand gestures. Consider for one moment that the person in the other car was a single mother with a very young child, and she was new to the area and trying to get her bearings. Your actions would undoubtedly frighten this person and add undue stress to an already stressful situation. In this situation it would be more appropriate and effective for you and the other person if this action was ignored, so as to avoid stress and remain calm, thus ensuring the situation did not escalate and preventing further complications and issues arising. In Theme 5, 'Conflict Resolution', you will find activities to use with young people to develop their skills and awareness in understanding which conflict resolution strategies they should use in different situations and in response to different issues.

Misunderstandings are often the root cause to girls' arguments and friendship disputes, which are escalated by the responses from each person caught up in the drama cycle. When a person says something innocently or without any malice intended, the reaction of the person this was directed toward can often cause rifts in friendship groups if her perception of the situation is skewed, or her self-worth is low, or if girls lack the emotional and social competencies required to effectively respond to situations which they perceive to be an attack upon them personally.

Take Lisa, a 14 year old who is one of many girls within her friendship circle. Within this circle of friends there are girls who are very close and would do everything together, and other girls who are a part of the circle, but who are on the fringes of the group and may spend time with the others outside of school only occasionally. Kate and Lisa were very close friends, and Kate would frequently sleep over at Lisa's house. On occasions, Kate would use Lisa's phone to text boys or speak to her parents. Lisa didn't like Kate using her phone, especially to text boys, who were often older and explicit in their use of language. She did not feel comfortable with them having her phone number, but was unsure of how to approach Kate to ask her to stop. After a period of weeks, Lisa had decided she had had enough, and when Kate took the phone from Lisa to send a text message, Lisa grabbed it back and pushed Kate away. The situation escalated, creating rifts within the friendship group as Kate sought revenge by making Lisa's life difficult. Others within their circle tried to resolve the issues by attempting to mediate between the two, but this bore little success on the situation because, as in many instances similar to this, the group became divided and sided with one party over the other. Behaviours escalated and culminated in Lisa being physically assaulted by Kate, leaving her with significant injuries.

It is important that girls are provided with an opportunity to learn and practise skills needed to express how they feel, communicate their needs, and to explain what they want without situations escalating to the point where they are fearful of attacks and are subjected to physical assaults from others.

Many schools now incorporate conflict resolution training into continuing professional education programmes and have provided in-depth training to staff to provide the skills required to facilitate discussions and overcome problems that may arise among young people. This is a progressive step for schools that recognize sanctions and punishments alone will not affect change in young people's behaviours and resolve what may be deep-rooted issues for some young people. Although training staff to manage incidents when they occur is a positive and proactive approach by schools to resolve conflicts and bullying, it can still fail to prevent problems from occurring in the first place. If we truly want to prevent conflict and bullying behaviours, we should be training young people in conflict resolution skills and those interpersonal skills every individual requires to ensure we communicate in an appropriate, positive and effective manner that prevents such issues from occurring in the first place or, when they do occur, to prevent the escalation of behaviours that ultimately have an adverse effect on all children and young people caught up in any conflict situation.

Conflict resolution skills are some of the most important tools we can pass onto young people. Every day we will find ourselves in some sort of conflict situation, either internally or externally – with ourselves as our actions clash with our values and needs, or with others whose actions are not meeting our needs. We can experience conflict directly through a disagreement with another person or indirectly through the misinterpretation of actions by others, or when forced to choose sides when friendships turn bad, for example. When contemplating conflict situations that may arise on a daily basis and considering the outcomes of these, we often find that the situation has not ended satisfactorily. The situation may have been left unresolved or will have escalated to a point where individuals involved are constantly arguing and may possibly lead to more serious incidents of physical assault.

When we are involved in conflict or bullying, we can respond in one of four ways in an effort to resolve it. All four responses have positive and negative outcomes depending on the situation, the way in which we deploy the response, and the expectation we have for resolution. Our thoughts and feelings in any given situation drive our actions; if these thoughts and feelings are negative, ultimately our responses to the situation will be negative, most commonly getting angry and acting aggressively towards the other person.

When responding to conflict or bullying, we do one of the following:

- *Avoid:* we avoid situations, events or places where we know conflict will occur; we may also avoid people we are in conflict with so we do not experience problems or arguments.

- *Deflect:* we act in a similar manner to our aggressor, or we direct our anger at the situation or towards others who may not necessarily be the one we are in conflict with; we may also use a facilitator to mediate between us and the person we are in conflict with to try to resolve the situation.

- *Confront:* we argue with the person we are in conflict with or use aggressive actions to state our view.

- *Ignore:* we act as if the problems do not exist or ignore the person with whom we are in conflict.

When choosing which method to use to resolve our conflict, we often revert to past experiences or observed behaviours. Our thoughts and feelings during the period of conflict will also dictate our responses and behaviours. If our needs are not being met and the situation presented to us is reinforcing negative internal thinking and judgements we make about ourselves, it can be difficult to constructively respond to conflict to successfully achieve a positive outcome for all parties involved. Figure 6.2 illustrates how our internal thoughts and behaviours overlap with the methods we use to respond to conflict and bullying, which in turn affects our behaviours in any given situation.

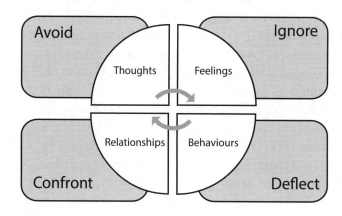

Figure 6.2: Responding to conflict

Resolving conflict

If we find ourselves in conflict, it is often a result of others not meeting our needs or acting in a way that conflicts with our needs. As Marshall B. Rosenberg (2003, p.132) states: 'Whenever we imply that someone [or something] is wrong or bad, what we are really saying is that she or he is not acting in harmony with our needs.' Our thoughts and feelings at the time of conflict will directly impact upon the methods we use for resolution and the behaviours we portray as a means of applying a resolution to the problem. Refer back to the situation with Kate and Lisa and the phone: Lisa's need for respect and understanding were not being met by Kate. As a result, Lisa was feeling extremely frustrated and hurt, often thinking that she did not have the authority to tell Kate not to use her phone, and fretful that she did not have the courage to communicate her feelings. This left her feeling angry, as well as inferior and guilty that she was questioning their friendship, leading her to ultimately confront Kate using negative actions driven by her feelings and thoughts of anger, guilt, inferiority and hurt, which resulted in the situation escalating to inevitably incur physical violence.

The method we choose to resolve any given conflict or bullying situation can have positive or negative outcomes, dependent on the thoughts and feelings driving the behaviours we present. Understanding when our needs are not being met and the impact this has upon our thoughts and feelings will allow us to respond more effectively to difficult situations. As adults, we can find it quite difficult to rationalize our thoughts in this way because of the years of programming that has taught us to respond very differently to our thoughts and feelings, often to push those feelings further within us and cause us more internal pain as we avoid expressing our anxieties and concerns. Adults will often find it very difficult to recognize their own feelings when presented with different situations; so how, then, can young people be expected to manage their behaviours, friendships, emotions and thoughts when some adults find this a difficult task?

Teaching girls to recognize when the actions of others may not coexist in harmony with their own needs and values can be challenging. But educating young women to apply this thinking in their relationships, both romantic and platonic, can be positive and rewarding. Being able to understand and manage their own emotions and thoughts as a means of managing their relationships with others is the first step towards achieving healthy friendships and building self-esteem, self-respect and confidence. This in turn leads to emotionally balanced women who are able to apply themselves academically and socially.

The role of language in relationships

Managing thoughts and feelings is only the first step towards achieving equilibrium in young girls' relationships. The language and behaviours used by young people, and many adults, when responding to negative situations can often trigger conflict and bullying. When responding to these situations, girls often use language and a tone of voice that can inadvertently be interpreted negatively by others. When girls express that they are frustrated, hurt, annoyed or upset by the actions of others, they may place blame on that person, who in turn may feel resentful that they have not been listened to or have been treated unfairly. Young women often state that the problems they are experiencing started with a small and inconsequential incident that resulted in one person saying something that was misinterpreted by others.

Coinciding with teaching students to understand their needs and values, and manage their thoughts and feelings when these are not being met, it is important to teach girls how to use effective, positive and non-threatening language when communicating with others. Very often girls are quick to place blame and express anger towards others if they have caused them harm in any way. Marshall B. Rosenberg (2003, p.19) observes that, 'Communication is life-alienating when it clouds our awareness that we are each responsible for our own thoughts, feelings, and actions.' Young girls are quick to blame their friends for the way they feel and think and often refer to the actions of their friends for causing them harm. This way of thinking is not limited to young women; often adults find it difficult to comprehend that they, and only they, are responsible for their thoughts and feelings. It can be very limiting when we place our happiness in the hands of others. Consider for one moment what it feels like when a romantic relationship ends and who gets the blame for our thoughts and feelings. Negative thoughts and feelings are often directed toward the other person for the relationship not working out, and they are blamed for ending the romance. Our focus is often on the actions of others as the problem, and as such, the language we use to communicate with them is often accusatory and angry, which in turn causes tensions and problems to arise.

Young girls experience a range of social and emotional issues when they are involved in bullying relationships, and these issues are often important underlying drivers for the way in which they respond to each other. Often, if a young person does not 'fit in' with the perceived ideal of the group, such as not wearing the right clothing or partaking in certain social events, they can find themselves ostracized by the group. Keeping up with social expectations can have a huge strain on an individual's emotional and mental health. Responding effectively to the social and emotional issues raised in friendship circles is dependent on how girls themselves are able to manage their feelings and behaviour. A young girl who lacks self-respect, self-esteem and confidence will inevitably respond negatively to the social and emotional issues arising in her peer group and she may take on the issues as a direct, personal attack. Being able to express her thoughts and feelings about given situations in a manner that is non-threatening, but assertive, can make the difference between resolving issues positively as they arise or escalating to situations where bullying behaviours become the norm in the friendship circle.

When problems arise in girls' friendship groups, attempts can be made by members of the peer group to manage and contain the bullying by trying to mediate between the two parties, in the face of no other effective intervention to prevent it escalating. This can cause more problems within girl groups and create a ripple effect as more peers are dragged into the drama cycle. Intervention by adults often comes as the problems have reached a point of destruction and friendship groups are in turmoil. Work to repair the harm can cause more issues as the root causes of the problem are not explored and adults respond only to the immediate concerns presented. Where the root causes are not explored, and no attempt is made to resolve the real issues present in the friendship group, problems often spiral out of control, and although the solutions put in place appear to have resolved the issue presented to adults, they serve only to increase tensions between individuals. This is often the result of one party being apportioned blame for the problems and the other party not taking ownership of their role within the dispute. As a result, the resolution often leaves more problems in its wake than it solves.

Occasionally, efforts are made to teach young people how to communicate with others about their thoughts and feelings without causing conflict to arise. This training is often provided to young people who volunteer to become peer mentors within school. Peer mentors are taught to communicate with others using 'I' statements rather than 'you' statements as a means of positively and effectively communicating their thoughts and feelings with others without causing conflict. This means of communicating should be passed onto our younger generation; adults have a responsibility to be positive role models to children and young people, but all too often, adults instead are responsible for passing onto others their own feelings of frustration and annoyance towards young people through the language they use. Compounding the problem, language becomes accusatory when the child is blamed for adults' feelings of frustration and anger. Adults can often be heard blaming their class or children for their feelings of exhaustion or frustration, but they should understand that they are the ones responsible for these feelings through the thoughts they generate when children misbehave or fail to conform to their expectations. The blame they apportion to children can be heard in the statements they make to other adults and children, where they may use such phrases as 'You are not listening' or 'You are being disobedient.' If an adult entered into a classroom reflectively, thinking positively about situations, they would be less likely to feel frustrated if the class were not performing to their expectations. This in turn can be reflected in the language they use when responding to the class: 'I feel frustrated when I try to help you complete your work, and you don't listen.' This places responsibility for the completion of work with the child and reduces any stress the adult may experience without escalating the situation to cause conflict between adult and child. Modelling this reflective language to young people benefits them in two ways: first, they observe a means of communicating that positively resolves disputes, and second, it allows them to reflect on their responsibility in any given situation.

Communicating effectively and positively should not be something that is taught to the minority. Effective communication should underlie everything we teach our children and not become a stand-alone item in training programmes. Modelling the use of effective communication helps young people to observe and re-enact respectful and positive ways of communicating their feelings and thoughts towards others without causing conflict. Activities can be found in Themes 1, 4 and 5 to assist you with teaching young people to communicate their feelings and thoughts effectively and positively to get their needs met.

Chapter 7

Using this Resource

Understanding and eradicating girl bullying is a complex and multifaceted undertaking, and while many educators may see the need for a reduction in female conflict in their school, the needs of the individual girls are often usurped by the blanket needs of the wider school community, often born of necessity from too-tight budgets, time constraints and a bulging curriculum. While this is an understandable position, without a concentrated, planned curriculum and approach, the ripples of discord and conflict will only further gather force until educators are drowning under a sea of relationship issues that are preventing teaching and learning from taking place.

What must be of most importance to all members of the school community is a student's ability to learn, study and graduate from school successfully, to the best of their ability, without hindrance from outside influences. However, when we think back to our own time at school and that of our family and friends, we begin to understand the importance of spending our formative years in a warm, nurturing, reflective community that builds skills and awareness, as well as a competency to pass exams.

With this in mind, *Surviving Girlhood* and the activities included are designed to build students' awareness, social skills, emotional literacy and critical thinking skills alongside developing their esteem and confidence through exploration of what it means to be in relationship with themselves and others. The activities have been designed for girls aged 11–16 years, but can work just as well with boys and with older or younger students, with a slight change of language as necessary. Educators are encouraged to use their discretion and identify activities that will best reflect the needs of their students while not being afraid to challenge girls to explore difficult thoughts, feelings and concepts.

These activities can be used for individual students with an identified need, in a small or larger group setting as character education building, in an after-school programme, or for a whole class. Each activity is cross-referenced to the main themes so teachers can also create a hand-picked session-by-session curriculum of activities.

The five themes

The activities and resources span five themes which explore the dynamic of female relationships and development of inner awareness. The themes can be explored in isolation or as a continued programme of work, as each theme builds on the preceding one. Throughout the themes, students are encouraged to reflect on their thoughts, feelings, needs and values, as this is central to the programme. All activities are designed to be reflective and discussion-based in a responsive, open classroom.

- *Being Me* explores our individual needs and values to build self-esteem, self-awareness and emotional literacy. Activities explore how we relate to ourselves and others, and how we define who we are.

- *Influences* explores how the world around us impacts our thoughts, feelings and behaviour, including peer and social influences. Activities explore how and why we are influenced and build media literacy to encourage students to be discerning technology users.

- *Respect, Responsibilities, Relationships* explores our rights and responsibilities and the balance between respect for self and others. Activities explore developing girls' awareness of the importance of self-respect to foster respectful behaviour towards others, defining healthy boundaries and accepting social responsibilities.

- *Managing Relationships* develops students' awareness of friendships, exploring appropriate conduct for meeting their own social needs, including those in romantic relationships, in positive and appropriate ways.

- *Conflict Resolution* builds on the growing awareness of students with skills and techniques to manage relationship difficulties when they occur and develop empathy and understanding for the needs of others.

The role of the teacher

The task of teaching social and emotional skills or providing character education programmes is sadly all too often relegated to the member of staff least likely to complain or it is passed from person to person to teach. While a full curriculum or a lack of trained staff and resources are often to blame, in reality 'character education' (developing young people's social and emotional awareness) should be a constant endeavour, as opportunities exist in every subject and throughout every part of the day – as students come in to school in the morning, study characters from nineteenth-century literature, eat lunch, undertake algebraic problems and play sport. To truly shift the school climate away from an atmosphere of negativity and conflict to an open, reflective community in relationship, a shift in awareness and approach is naturally needed.

However, as any well-meaning, enthusiastic teacher may encounter, trying to change a pervasive cross-cultural attitude through one person's actions alone can be difficult. This resource and activities may not revolutionize the dynamic in your school but may assist in changing girls' behaviour and attitudes to create harmony, positive relationships and success – now and in their future lives.

As demoralizing as it may feel being a lone voice of change in a sea of resistance, what is crucial to remember is the effect each person can have, perhaps just on one other. By exploring, testing, using and developing the activities included here, it is our hope that we grow teachers who are more reflective, open, empathic and aware, so they can assist students to grow likewise.

The activities within the five themes are designed to be reflective and to promote conversation. Many of the activities ask girls to look within themselves and reflect on their true thoughts and feelings, which can be a risky proposal for young women who are more used to suppressing their needs and painting on a brave face of indifference, attitude and aggression. Creating a safe space is crucial for encouraging any work at depth, yet this may take some time to develop as the programme continues.

As the teacher or facilitator, your role of absolute importance is to set the tone in the room and the expectations for attitude and behaviour. Activity 1.1 refers to creating a class or group agreement to encourage appropriate, respectful behaviour, but it is worth remembering the power of modelling to students attributes, such as:

- Practising good manners.

- Showing respect.

- Setting appropriate boundaries.

- Challenging and being challenged.

- Enquiring and being interested in the thoughts and opinions of others.

- Exhibiting emotional literacy, utilizing an emotional vocabulary, reflecting on and communicating with feeling.

- Encouraging discussion and debate.

- Modelling empathy and openness.

There are many ways to create a safe and emotionally open classroom, modelling the principles highlighted above. Some methods include:

- Acknowledging and greeting students by name as they enter the room.

- Smiling.

- Meeting people's eyes.

- Asking, not expecting, students to do something for you (for example, asking if a student wants to run an errand, not telling them to do so).

- Saying please and thank you.

- Getting on to a student's level when in conversation (for example, if they are sitting at a desk, crouching down or sitting with them).

- Using paraphrasing and reflective techniques to communicate that you understood and heard what a student told you.

- Admitting and communicating your own feelings (for example, 'I feel really disappointed that you didn't do your homework').

- Owning thoughts and feelings as opposed to making blanket statements, through the use of 'I' think, feel, want, etc.

- Using minimal encouragers, such as 'Go on' or 'Tell me more', to encourage discussion.

- Being empathic by reflecting on the needs and feelings of others (for example, 'It must have hurt you to be left out in that situation').

- Asking for clarification instead of assuming.

- Offering your own thoughts and opinions, when appropriate, to contribute to the reflective sharing process.

- Being consistent with thought, word and deed.

- Arranging the classroom to be appropriate for the activity (for example, not sitting students in rows when undertaking a discussion-based activity).

- Avoiding the use of sarcasm, criticism, personal and potentially hurtful remarks to students, humiliation, punishment in front of others, any form of retribution, and singling students out in a negative sense.

Questions to ask ourselves

Developing our own relationship with ourselves and others can be an insightful and rewarding process that enhances our classroom practice and personal lives. Asking great questions can often reveal great answers!

Consider the following questions about your practice and your students.

Questions about you

- Why did you enter the teaching profession or the field of education?

- What do you consider to be your skills and talents?

- What do you feel are your most important needs that are fulfilled through your career?

- What do you feel are other important needs you have in life that should be met on a regular basis? (The questionnaire in Worksheet 2: Needs Quiz, may help you to identify these.)

- Where are your needs currently being met?

- Which needs might be unmet or in conflict?

- What do you model to students on a day-to-day basis?

Questions about your students

- What skills and attributes do you hope your students will leave school with?

- What thought do you hope your students leave your classroom with each day?

- What is the overall emotional climate in your classroom and school?

- Are your students' needs being met on a day-to-day basis?

- Do your students generally feel valued, accepted, heard and understood?

- Are there opportunities for your students to develop strong relationships with others?

- Do students have opportunities to communicate their thoughts and feelings to someone who will listen?

Continued professional development, self-study and reflective teaching practices will all help to inform our practice, communication and the curriculum we offer to our students. However, in a connected world of relationships there is no limit to the importance of warmth, humility, friendly words and a smile – things we often seem to have forgotten to provide for our children and young people.

Part 2

Activities

Theme 1

Being Me

Ground Rules

Resources required:	*Large sheet of paper*
	Marker pens
Learning objective:	*To establish group ground rules*

Explain to students the importance of creating a safe, open and respectful environment in which to work, particularly when discussing issues such as friendships and bullying.

Highlight the importance of creating a set of ground rules or promises that everyone can stick to – including you, the facilitator, in this and every other session. Ask students to suggest some promises and, as a group, decide on the ones that are most important.

Record these on a large sheet of paper, and once completed, ask everyone (yourself included) to sign their name to indicate their agreement. Post this sheet of paper somewhere prominent in the room and ensure that it is available for every session to refer back to.

Some ideas for promises are:

- To respect one another.
- Only one person will speak at a time.
- There are no such things as bad ideas.
- Treat everyone as an equal.
- Get involved and participate.

DISCUSSION POINTS

- *How can we make sure these promises are more than just words?*
- *How does it feel when someone treats you this way? For example, if someone shows you respect?*
- *What does the word 'respect' mean to you?*

Facilitator notes

- This activity can set the tone for the entire programme. Ensure that ideas are generated from students rather than laid down by you. The more that students are involved, the more likely they will stick to their promises.
- Think about the language you use – 'promises' sounds a lot more cooperative and cohesive than 'rules'.
- Ensure that you make it clear that the promises are also for you to stick to. You may wish to ask students to suggest one or two promises specifically for you, such as promising to try to make sessions interesting or promising to listen to students' ideas.

Understanding Needs

Resources required: *None*

Learning objectives: *To begin to explore the concept of human needs, including needs which are physical and emotional*

Begin by explaining that this activity will focus on exploring the needs human beings have, some of which are essential, like food, and some are personal, such as a need for expressing ourselves through the clothes we wear.

Discuss with the students some of the different needs we have, writing the answers on the board. Refer to the promises agreement from Activity 1.1 to ensure answers are appropriate and respectful.

Some ideas of needs may be:

- food
- water
- sleep
- fun
- friendship
- exercise
- being creative
- being independent.

DISCUSSION POINTS 1

- *Which needs are essential? (For example, food, water, rest.)*
- *Which needs are common to all of us?*
- *Which needs are much more personal to us and differ from person to person? (For example, some people have a need to have their space and be quiet and alone, while others have a need to always be surrounded by people.)*

Of the list on the board, ask students which needs they would consider to be physical and which they think are emotional.

DISCUSSION POINTS 2

- *Which needs are more important, physical or emotional?*
- *What happens when our physical needs are not met?*
- *What happens when our emotional needs are not met?*
- *Are there any unhelpful or unhealthy ways people try to get their needs met?*

Maslow's Hierarchy of Needs

> **Resources required:** *Large sheets of paper*
>
> *Marker pens*
>
> *Copies of Worksheet 1: Maslow's Triangle – one per group*
>
> **Learning objectives:** *To understand the different levels of need, and to explore what happens when needs are not met*

Draw a triangle on the board to represent Maslow's Hierarchy of Needs and introduce the idea of having many different types of needs, starting with essential needs at the bottom of the triangle. Share the titles of the different levels of need as you write them into the triangle:

- essential human needs
- safety
- love and belonging
- self-esteem
- purpose and meaning to life.

As a whole group, brainstorm some needs which may fit into each category, e.g.:

- Essential human needs – water, food, shelter.
- Safety – physical safety, safe place to live and work, feeling confident and secure.
- Love and belonging – family, friendship, relationships.
- Self-esteem – feeling confident, self-respect, looking and feeling good.
- Purpose and meaning to life – through career, work, music, religion, being adventurous.

Split students into groups of five or six and give each group a large sheet of paper and some marker pens. Ask students to re-create the triangle on the board with five different levels (you may wish to have this prepared ahead of time). On their sheet of paper, ask students to work together to write in the different levels of the triangle as many different needs as they can think of, reminding them to consider both physical and emotional needs. Once completed, give feedback and share some ideas of each group.

Give each group another large sheet of paper and ask them to repeat the exercise, this time writing in each level of the triangle what might happen when those needs are *not met*. Provide students with an example, such as what happens when people don't get their need for safety met: they feel frightened, they cannot concentrate, and they become stressed. Share the answers and discuss some examples of situations that might leave people without their needs being met, such as the person being bullied not having his need for safety met when in school.

Facilitator notes

- This can be a difficult idea for some students to comprehend, so provide plenty of examples, and provide the groups with a copy of Maslow's Triangle (Worksheet 1) as necessary.

Activity 1.4

Exploring My Needs

Resources required: *Copies of Worksheet 2: Needs Quiz – one per person*

Copies of Worksheet 3: Needs Cards – one set

Learning objective: *To begin to explore individual needs*

Distribute copies of Worksheet 2: Needs Quiz to the students and ask them to complete the quiz individually. It is important to stress that there are no right or wrong answers and everyone's results will vary: it is about exploring their personality and identifying what is important to them.

Facilitator notes

- It is important to stress to students to be as honest as possible in completing the quiz.

- Depending on the age and ability level of your students, you may wish to read the questions aloud and have everyone complete the answers together so that you can explain or expand on any of the questions as necessary.

When completed, students should score their quiz as described on the final page and identify their top three needs.

DISCUSSION POINTS

- *Was anyone surprised at their top three needs?*

- *Can anyone describe the ways in which they meet one of their top needs?*

- *Does anyone feel as though one of their top needs are not being met at the moment?*

- *How does that affect you?*

Finally, gather students in a circle and reiterate the importance of sticking to the promises made in Activity 1.1. You may wish to add additional directions for circle work, such as using a talking object to help with taking turns in speaking and listening.

Spread the Needs Cards from Worksheet 3 face up in the middle of the circle and ask students to spend a few moments looking at them. Explain that they will choose one card to describe something they need from everyone else to be able to work at their best in this class or group.

When everyone is ready, move around the circle asking each person to share their need. Time allowing, students may wish to share why that need is important to them and how others could meet this need.

Needs Case Studies

Resources required:	*Copies of Worksheet 4: Emotional Needs Scenarios – one per person or one per small group*
Learning objectives:	*To begin to explore the consequences of meeting our needs in healthy and unhealthy ways*

Introduce the activity by reminding students of the different types of needs – some are essential, some are physical and some are emotional. This activity will be focusing on emotional needs that relate to our personalities.

Distribute copies of Worksheet 4: Emotional Needs Scenarios individually, or split students into small groups to complete this task.

Ask students to read the three scenarios and complete the questions about what these young people may need and how they can meet their emotional needs more positively and appropriately.

DISCUSSION POINTS

• *What is Jenny doing to try to meet her need for friendship and to feel included?*

• *Has anyone ever been in a similar situation to Mark? What did you need at that time?*

• *What could Emma do to meet her needs in a more positive way?*

Needs versus Wants

Introduce the topic of wants and needs. Explain the difference between the two:

- *Wants are things that you desire a lot.*

- *Needs are things necessary for your life.*

Explain that every individual has the same basic needs, but the things we want may differ.

Distribute the Worksheet 5: Wants or Needs? In pairs or small groups, students should decide which items are wants and which are needs.

Go through the answers as a whole class. Ask students if they can think of any other needs that humans may have. Write a list of the things that students might need and want on the board.

DISCUSSION POINTS 1

- *How do we feel if we don't get what we need to live?*
  - *When we are hungry and have no food?*
  - *When we don't feel safe?*
  - *When we are not accepted by others?*

- *Is this different from how we feel when we don't get what we want or desire?*
  - *The latest fashion or technology?*

- *What happens when some people always get what they want while others don't get anything or little of what they want?*
  - *Greed, jealousy, crime, bullying, hate, segregation.*

Ask students if they can think of places or situations where needs might not be met, and list those on the board.

DISCUSSION POINTS 2

- *What happens when human rights, or needs, are not being met or are violated? (For example, segregation of communities, the Holocaust, intolerance, hatred.)*

Facilitator notes

- This exercise should ideally begin by looking at global issues, such as poverty, hunger, women's rights issues and life in war-torn countries. After discussion ask the students if they can think of any situations in their local area where basic human needs – our rights – may not be met. Discussions should look at poverty, young carers and bullying (where individuals feel unsafe or not accepted by peers).

- Ask the students to reflect on times they felt their needs were not being met.

Exploring My Values

Resources required: *Copies of Worksheet 6: Values List – one per pair*

Learning objective: *To begin to explore the concept of values*

Begin by discussing what we mean by something of value and what a personal value is (e.g. something that we hold dear to us or that is of importance for us). Ask students to identify a few things they value and write them on the board – many of these are likely to be physical things, such as phones and MP3 players.

Share with students the idea that physical things we want or value represent something else; for example, our clothes might represent our style and individuality. Our MP3 players might represent a love of music and creativity, while for someone else, their MP3 player is a way for them to get the solitude and privacy they need when they put their headphones in their ears.

Place students into pairs and ask them to work together to:

- Make a list of all the things that are important to them.

- Go through the list and match them with values, using Worksheet 6: Values List if needed.

Our values drive us and shape our lives and the decisions we make. Someone who values peace and quiet probably won't choose to work in a loud factory. Someone who values being creative and artistic might feel unhappy with an office job.

DISCUSSION POINTS

- *What do you value most?*

- *Can anyone think of how that value has influenced a decision they've made?*

- *Can anyone think of a time when they have gone against something they valued, such as valuing honesty and telling a lie? How did it feel?*

Valuing Role Models

Resources required: *White paper*

Marker pens

Copies of Worksheet 6: Values List – one per small group

Sticky notes

Poster tack

Learning objectives: *To identify people who live by their values*

Remind students what a value is – something that is important to us and shapes the way we live our lives. Give students some examples of values or ask them to identify some, and write these on the board (e.g. beauty, independence, honesty, respect, security, etc.).

Discuss some of the most important values we see in the people we admire, such as our role models, friends and family. Ask for some examples of role models and what they might value, such as an Olympic athlete valuing determination or strength.

As a whole group, come up with a list of 10–12 main values (using copies of Worksheet 6: Values List, if necessary). Ask students to write these main values on pieces of paper (one per sheet) and stick them to the walls. Hand out some sticky notes to each person, and give them five minutes to think of anyone whose lives reflect the values on the wall.

Ask students to write the person's name on the sticky note and stick it onto the value. They might be a celebrity, a friend, teacher, family member or someone they've heard about on TV or in the news.

Once everyone has had time to distribute their sticky notes, ask each person to share at least one name they stuck to a value and to describe how that person lives that value.

DISCUSSION POINTS

- *Where do our values come from?*

- *What value might people admire in you?*

- *What happens when we are surrounded by people who don't match our values? (For example, if we value honesty and one of our friends is always spreading gossip and telling lies.)*

Guessing Values

Resources required:	*Copies of Worksheet 6: Values List – one per pair*
	Sticky notes
Learning objective:	*To understand how our values influence our decisions and actions*

Split students into pairs and ask one person to be 'A' and the other 'B'.

Ask the As to choose a value from Worksheet 6: Values List, write it on a Sticky note and stick it onto their partner's forehead without Person B seeing what's written.

Person B can ask ten questions to guess what their value is, but person A can answer only yes or no. When Person B has asked their ten questions, they can guess what they think their value is.

As and Bs can then swap over and repeat.

Facilitator notes

Depending on the age and ability level of your students, they may need some help in thinking of questions to ask their partner to help them guess what it is they value. You may wish to do a whole-group example first or write some sample questions on the board, such as:

- Do I like to travel a lot? (Adventurous, independent)

- Do I like to spend time on my own? (Peace, solitude)

- Am I always wearing the latest fashions? (Beauty, creativity)

- Am I always hanging out in a big crowd? (Belonging, friendship)

Values Pie Chart

Resources required: *Rolls of masking tape*

Sheets of white paper

Marker pens

Learning objective: *To explore the value we place on different strengths*

Use masking tape to create a large eight-spoke wheel on the floor. Place eight pieces of paper with one of the following values written on them in each section of the wheel.

Share with the group that this wheel will represent some of the main strengths we value in ourselves and others. Discuss as a group the eight main values:

- appearance or looks
- intelligence
- creativity
- self-respect
- sense of humour
- trustworthiness
- popularity
- confidence.

Gather students around the circle, and instruct them that they will be voting with their feet by jumping to stand in one section of the wheel to indicate the importance they place on these different values. Ask students which value they think is most important:

- For a friend to have.
- To develop in themselves.
- For a romantic partner to have.

Discuss what they feel is the least important strength of value for a friend, a boyfriend or romantic partner to have, and to develop in themselves. Time and space allowing, give each student some masking tape, and ask them to work individually to make their own wheel on the floor, this time representing eight things they value in themselves (these may be the same as, or different from the values above). Instruct students to use the tape to make each section of the wheel large or small depending on the importance they place on that value, like a pie chart. Students should write their eight values on pieces of paper and display them in each section of their wheel.

How do *You* Feel?

<table>
<tr><td>Resources required:</td><td>Worksheet 7: Feelings Scenarios – one copy</td></tr>
<tr><td></td><td>Four sheets of white paper</td></tr>
<tr><td></td><td>Marker pens</td></tr>
<tr><td></td><td>Sticky tape</td></tr>
<tr><td>Learning objectives:</td><td>To encourage students to consider their emotional responses and the consequences of their feelings</td></tr>
</table>

Write the words 'Angry', 'Scared', 'Upset' and 'Embarrassed' on four sheets of paper. Tape them to the wall in the four corners of the room and gather students in the middle or to one side.

Explain that you will read a statement aloud, and then they must consider how they would feel in that scenario. Students should 'vote with their feet' and go and stand in the corner of the room corresponding with how they think they would feel in that situation. For example, the statement is 'I just found out my best friend has spread a rumour about me, and now everyone is laughing at me'. Students should decide whether they would feel angry, scared, upset or embarrassed.

It is important to stress that there are no right or wrong answers: students should think about their own individual response, not just follow their friends!

DISCUSSION POINTS

During the activity, ask the students to reflect on the following:

- *What would be the consequence of your feeling – would you act on it?*

- *How would the situation be different if you chose a different feeling?*

- *Can you change the way you feel?*

- *Who is responsible for you feeling that way?*

- *Are you surprised people feel so differently about the same situation?*

The Wheel of Life

Resources required: *Copies of Worksheet 8: The Wheel of Life– one per person*

Marker pens

Learning objectives: *To build awareness of the importance of living a balanced life and to prompt students to begin to set goals toward positive change*

Give each student a copy of Worksheet 8: The Wheel of Life.

Explain that the wheel represents different areas of a person's life, such as family, friends, school and health. Discuss with students how just as it is important to eat a balanced diet, it is important to live an overall balanced life.

DISCUSSION POINTS

- *What would happen if we put all our efforts into making just one or two areas of our life perfect and neglect the rest?*

- *Can you think of any examples of how a person fails to lead a balanced life? (For example, someone who hangs around with their friends all the time and doesn't do any school work, or the workaholic adult who doesn't spend any time at home.)*

Students should consider each part of the wheel and give that area of their life a score from 1 to 10 to describe how happy or fulfilled they are in that life area, 1 being not happy at all and 10 being very happy.

Once complete, ask students to complete the area of the worksheet which asks them to identify the parts of their life they would like to improve and to identify three goals to help them do that within the next month and three goals within the next year.

Students can share their results and goals, if they feel comfortable to do so.

Air Your Dirty Laundry!

Resources required:	*Long piece of yarn or string*
	Plastic clothes pegs
	Small squares of card
	Pens
Learning objectives:	*To prompt students to reflect on their attitude, behaviour, and positive and negative interactions with others and the impact of these*

Facilitator notes

- You will need to tie a long piece of yarn or string across the classroom at waist height in preparation for this activity.

Ask students to work individually to consider all of the things they have done in the past week (or month, depending on the age and awareness level of the students) that have left them feeling good about themselves, and any things they have done which have left them feeling bad about themselves, either because of the consequence (i.e., what happened as a result) or because of the feeling it left them with, such as feeling embarrassed, ashamed, worried or angry. Students can also consider things they *didn't* do which made them feel good or bad, such as choosing not to skip school with their friends, or choosing not to tidy their bedroom when asked.

Ask students to write their good and bad events on separate pieces of card, anonymously. When ready students should peg their card onto the 'washing line' on the *right* side for positive things they have done and on the *left* side for negative things.

Once complete, discuss the following points:

DISCUSSION POINTS

- *Are there more good or bad things on the washing line?*

- *How does it feel to see all these?*

- *Were you aware that your good and bad feelings were the result of your actions this week?*

- *How does it make you feel about your behaviour and choices now?*

Who am I?

<table>
<tr><td>Resources required:</td><td>Copies of Worksheet 9: Scenarios – one per person</td></tr>
<tr><td></td><td>Pens</td></tr>
<tr><td>Learning objectives:</td><td>To build self-awareness, in particular awareness of behaviour when in different 'roles'</td></tr>
</table>

Give each student a copy of Worksheet 9: Scenarios and ask them to complete it individually. It is important to stress that no two students' answers will be the same, as we are all different and think and feel differently.

Students should consider their different roles as a student, daughter, friend, etc., and explore how they might act differently in each role or when in the company of others, such as when they are in school, with their friends, or at home with their family.

DISCUSSION POINTS

- *Did anyone notice they play quite different roles depending on who they are spending time with? (if they would like to share)*

- *How does it feel to be in these roles?*

- *In which role are you happiest? Why?*

- *Which one is the real you?*

- *Do you think we should try to be the same with everyone, no matter if we're with our friends, our teacher, or our parents, for example?*

- *What are you thinking when you're in each role?*

- *What are you feeling?*

Tear Down, Build Up

Resources required:	*Worksheet 10: Outline of a Person – one copy*
	Sticky tape
Learning objective:	*To explore the emotional effects of being a target for hurtful language*

Gather the students in a circle, and briefly discuss how and why people hurt others, in particular, how people use words to threaten, hurt and manipulate. Explore how people can feel when they are the target of verbal bullying, teasing and put-downs, encouraging students to reflect on personal experience, if they feel comfortable to do so.

Show the group the paper with an outline of a person, and explain that they should make comments in turn using mean, hurtful or aggressive language without using overly derogatory or disrespectful terms or profanity. Their comments should be within reason – you may wish to remind students that this is an activity and refer back to the ground rules created in Activity 1.1.

As students make their comments, tear a piece of paper off the sheet, placing it in front of you. The last comment should coincide with the last tear. Ask students to reflect on what the sheet now symbolizes – the person is broken, destroyed, torn up inside.

Now repeat the activity, asking students to offer words of reconciliation or support in turn, and as each comment is made, use the sticky tape to stick the sheet back together until it resembles a full sheet at the end.

Encourage students to reflect upon how the person has not been made whole even though we have tried to make amends – the effects of our words and actions can still clearly be seen. Encourage students to share any personal experiences of the words or actions of others that still stay with them to this day, or offer the example of people who were bullied in childhood still carrying the hurt and pain with them in adulthood. Encourage students to reflect on this and share their thoughts and opinions.

DISCUSSION POINTS

- *We often hear the phrase 'Sticks and stones may break my bones, but names will never hurt me.' Do you think this is true?*

- *How does verbal bullying affect a person?*

- *Is everything made better again by apologising for our actions and trying to make amends?*

- *What does this piece of paper now represent? (e.g. someone who has scars inside; has been broken; has been deeply affected by the comments of others, etc.)*

Facilitator notes
- This activity is suitable for students of all levels of ability and understanding by developing the discussion points and encouraging more or less debate.

Cognitive Behavioural Techniques (CBT)

> **Resources required:** *Copies of Worksheet 11: CBT Scenarios – one per person*
>
> *Pens*
>
> **Learning objectives:** *To use cognitive behavioural techniques (CBT) to explore patterns of thinking and behaviour*

Give each student a copy of Worksheet 11: CBT Scenarios, and ask them to work individually to read the scenarios and complete the boxes to determine what they would think and feel in each situation.

Facilitator notes

- Some students may need further explanation of what 'evidence' means when exploring evidencing their thinking, that is, exploring alternative conclusions and testing the reality of their assumptions. One example is provided on the worksheet.

Once complete, discuss some or all of the following points as a full group:

DISCUSSION POINTS

- *What happens when we take time to reflect on our thoughts and feelings about a situation?*

- *Did anyone recognize that their immediate thought about a situation might not be accurate or that there might be alternative ways to look at it?*

- *What might the people in the scenarios need?*

- *How can they get their needs met?*

- *What happens when people's needs are not met?*

- *Can anyone think of a situation when they jumped to a conclusion which wasn't true?*

Maslow's Hierarchy of Needs
Maslow's Triangle

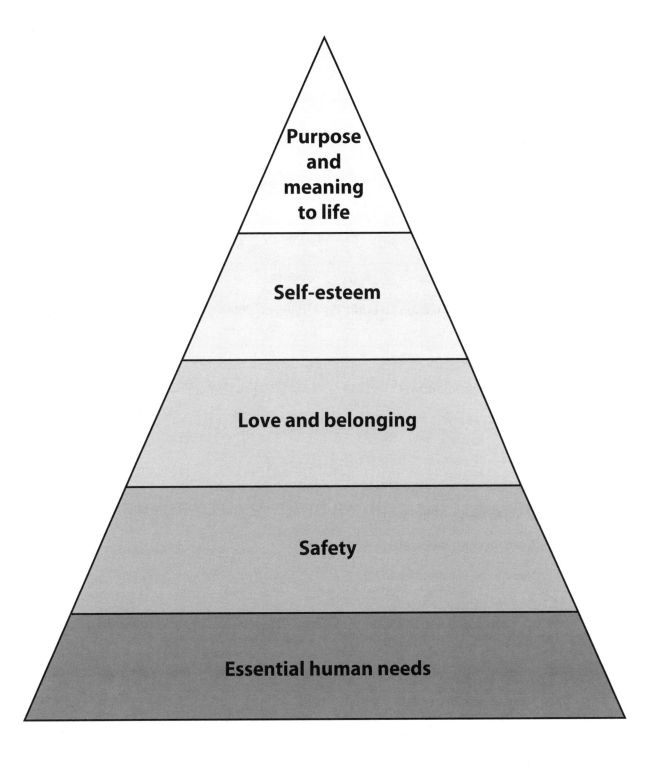

Exploring My Needs
Needs Quiz

Consider the following scenarios and think about what your underlying needs may be in these situations. These are the *needs* that drive your *behaviour*. Tick your top choice, if some of these scenarios do not apply to you, tick 'Does not apply' for those questions. When you have finished, add up the number of times you ticked each need to identify your top three.

Scenario 1

Your bedroom is an absolute mess, and you feel you have to tidy it before you can think about doing any homework:

a.	Need for balance	☐
b.	Need to be responsible/do the right thing	☐
c.	Does not apply	☐

Scenario 2

Your best friend asks for your opinion on an outfit she's trying on. It looks pretty awful on her, but you tell her she looks really nice in it:

a.	Need to be accepted/liked	☐
b.	Need for control/power	☐
c.	Does not apply	☐

Scenario 3

You hate it when your teacher yells at you for not doing your homework:

a.	Need to be heard/listened to	☐
b.	Need for control/power	☐
c.	Need to be accepted/liked	☐
d.	Does not apply	☐

Scenario 4

Your parents ask you to go with them to visit an elderly aunt, and you really don't want to go:

a.	Need to be independent/free	☐
b.	Need to be heard/listened to	☐
c.	Does not apply	☐

Scenario 5

You've been working on a group project for school with your friends, and when the teacher tells you she loves it, your friend takes all the credit, leaving you feeling angry:

a. Need to be heard/listened to ☐

b. Need to be appreciated/valued ☐

c. Need for control/power ☐

d. Does not apply ☐

Scenario 6

You feel cross and angry when people do things or make plans without your knowledge:

a. Need for control/power ☐

b. Need to be independent/free ☐

c. Does not apply ☐

Scenario 7

You feel upset and lonely when your friends don't include you in their plans:

a. Need to be accepted/liked ☐

b. Need to be appreciated/valued ☐

c. Does not apply ☐

Scenario 8

You can't sleep and feel anxious when you know you've got lots of homework and studying to do:

a. Need to achieve ☐

b. Need to be responsible/do the right thing ☐

c. Does not apply ☐

Scenario 9

You find yourself going along with your friends' ideas even when it doesn't feel right to you:

a. Need to be accepted/liked ☐

b. Need for peace/harmony ☐

c. Need for safety/security ☐

d. Does not apply ☐

Scenario 10

You find yourself eating when you're not even hungry:

- a. Need for safety/security ☐
- b. Need to be accepted/liked ☐
- c. Does not apply ☐

Scenario 11

You're having a disagreement with a friend, and they won't let you speak to get your point across, leaving you feeling frustrated and annoyed:

- a. Need to be heard/listened to ☐
- b. Need for peace/harmony ☐
- c. Need to be accepted/liked ☐
- d. Does not apply ☐

Scenario 12

You don't like teachers who are very bossy:

- a. Need for control/power ☐
- b. Need to be independent/free ☐
- c. Need for peace/harmony ☐
- d. Does not apply ☐

Scenario 13

It bothers you when your friends don't do nice things for you, even though you make loads of effort for them:

- a. Need to be appreciated/valued ☐
- b. Need for balance ☐
- c. Need to be accepted/liked ☐
- d. Does not apply ☐

Scenario 14

You hate being interrupted when you're speaking:

- a. Need for control/power ☐
- b. Need to be heard/listened to ☐
- c. Need to be appreciated/valued ☐
- d. Does not apply ☐

Scenario 15

The thought of having a boyfriend or girlfriend scares you:

- a. Need to be independent/free ☐
- b. Need for safety/security ☐
- c. Need to be accepted/liked ☐
- d. Does not apply ☐

Scenario 16

The thought of having to move to a new school terrifies you:

- a. Need for safety/security ☐
- b. Need for control/power ☐
- c. Does not apply ☐

Scenario 17

It really upsets you when your parents fight and argue:

- a. Need for peace/harmony ☐
- b. Need for safety/security ☐
- c. Does not apply ☐

Scenario 18

You feel guilty if you don't do any school work all weekend and just have fun with friends:

- a. Need for balance ☐
- b. Need to be responsible/do the right thing ☐
- c. Need to achieve ☐
- d. Does not apply ☐

Scenario 19

You've already planned out what you're going to study in college and what job you want to do – basically the next ten years of your life:

- a. Need to achieve ☐
- b. Need to be responsible/do the right thing ☐
- c. Need for safety/security ☐
- d. Does not apply ☐

Scenario 20

If your friends are picking on someone, you'll join in too:

a.   Need for control/power ☐

b.   Need to be accepted/liked ☐

c.   Need for safety/security ☐

d.   Does not apply ☐

Now it's time to add up your answers! Go back and count each time you ticked one of the ten needs below, writing the total number next to the need. Then list your top three needs at the end.

Balance _____

To be accepted/liked _____

Peace/harmony _____

Safety/security _____

To be responsible/do the right thing _____

To be appreciated/valued _____

To be heard/listened to _____

Control/power _____

To be independent/free _____

Achieve _____

My top three needs are:

_____

_____

_____

Exploring My Needs
Needs Cards

Support	**Acceptance**
Humour	**Care**
A Listening Ear	**Independence**
Peace	**Harmony**
Respect	**Fun**

Appreciation	**Freedom**
Compassion	**Inclusion**
Empathy	**Understanding**
Cooperation	**Inspiration**
Joy	**Hope**
Honesty	**Trust**

Warmth	Space
Inspiration	Creativity
Challenge	Participation
Belonging	Protection

Needs Case Studies
Emotional Needs Scenarios

Read the three scenarios and decide what these people may need. Remember, our needs are what drive our behaviour and are based on our feelings. Needs can be essential, physical or emotional. These scenarios deal with *emotional needs*.

Scenario 1

Jenny has been best friends with Sarah and Sophie since she was six years old. Now aged 13, they are as close as friends could be and do everything together. When a new girl joins their class, Sarah and Sophie are quick to include her, and before long she's a part of their group. Jenny begins to feel pushed out. She is sure that the three of them are doing things without her on the weekend, and she's sure they're laughing at her behind her back. Jenny feels so jealous that she's debating spreading some nasty rumours about the new girl and trying to push her out of their group.

What might be the needs that are driving Jenny's feelings and behaviour? (For example, a need to be accepted.)

_____

_____

What can Jenny do to meet her needs more positively and appropriately?

_____

_____

Scenario 2

Mark feels as though his science teacher, Mr Brown, is singling him out and picking on him. Mr Brown keeps asking him the toughest questions and makes him look stupid in front of the whole class. He always seems to be on his case, and last week he shouted at him and threw him out of the class for forgetting his homework. In a moment of anger, Mark thinks he will get his revenge by creating a hate website about Mr Brown. He posts the site online and encourages everyone to comment. Soon, the whole school is saying horrible things about Mr Brown on the site and laughing at him.

What may be some of the underlying needs that Mark has that are causing him to feel and act this way? (For example, a need to be heard and listened to.)

_____

_____

What can Mark do to meet his needs more positively and appropriately?

_____

_____

Scenario 3

Recently, Emma and her parents have not been seeing eye-to-eye. It feels to Emma that her dad is always getting at her and won't let her have any freedom. She can't go out with her friends on a Friday night, and they insist she has to be in bed before 10p.m., making her feel like a baby. Emma gets so fed up that she sneaks out on Saturday night to go to a party. When her parents find out, they ground her for a month.

What may be some of the underlying needs that Emma has that are causing her to feel and act this way? (For example, a need for freedom.)

_____

_____

What can Emma do to meet her needs more positively and appropriately?

_____

_____

Think about your needs. What do you need in these following scenarios?

When you fail a test at school, you need: _____

When you have an argument with family, you need: _____

When you fall out with your best friend, you need: _____

When your friends do something without you, you need: _____

When your parents are arguing, you need: _____

Needs versus Wants
Wants or Needs

Wants are things that you desire a lot.
Needs are things necessary for your life.

Which of the following are wants and which are needs?

		Want or need
Clean air		
Education		
A computer		
Branded clothes		
Nutritious food		

		Want or need
Fast food		
Holidays		
Shelter		
Safety		
Technology		
Cosmetic surgery		
Make-up		
Acceptance/love		

Exploring My Values
Values List

Choose five of the words below that describe the things you value the most in your life.

Which of these things are most important to you?

Write your values underneath and order them from 1 to 5, with 1 being the thing you value most.

Pleasure   Truth   Nature

Community   Excellence   Beauty

Health   Fitness   Religion   Love

Friendship   Achievement   Peace

Competition   Loyalty   Commitment   Honesty

Education   Adventure   Fulfilment   Wisdom

Creativity   Security   Freedom   Confidence

Trust   Money   Independence

Empowerment   Balance   Happiness

List your five top values in order of importance:

1. _____

2. _____

3. _____

4. _____

5. _____

How do *You* Feel?
Feelings Scenarios

Read the following scenarios aloud to the group, and ask them to 'vote with their feet' to describe how they would feel in each situation. Students should go and stand near the corresponding feeling (using the written feelings labels).

Scenario 1

I just found out my best friend has spread a rumour about me, and now everyone is laughing at me.

Scenario 2

I came bottom of the class in a test, and the teacher read out the results so everyone knows.

Scenario 3

My friends went out without me this weekend, without even inviting me.

Scenario 4

An older boy pushed me in the corridor earlier, and everyone laughed.

Scenario 5

My dad is making me clean my room, when all I want to do is watch TV.

Scenario 6

My parents have just told me we're moving house, and I will have to go to a new school.

Scenario 7

The class bully keeps targeting me, pushing and getting at me all the time.

Scenario 8

A girl in my science class keeps giving me dirty looks.

Scenario 9

I tripped up and nearly fell over in front of everyone outside school.

Scenario 10

My best friend has just started dating the person I really like.

The Wheel of Life

The eight sections in the Wheel of Life represent eight different aspects of your life, such as home and school. Think about each part of your life and mark on the line how satisfied you are, from 0 in the middle of the wheel, to 10 on the outside. When you have marked all eight sections, draw a line from each mark you've made to make a 'circle'.

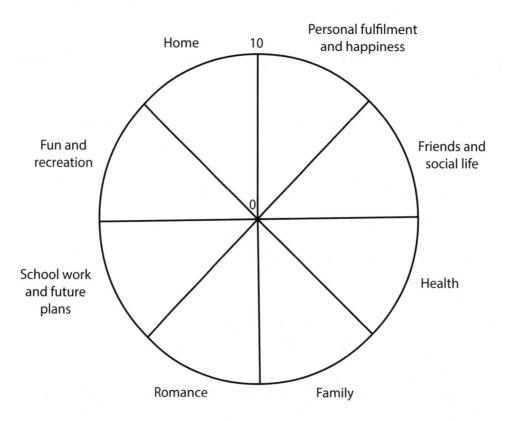

How in or out of balance is your life? How bumpy would the ride be if this were a real wheel?

My three main goals for the next month:	My three main goals for the next year:
1.	1.
2.	2.
3.	3.

Who am I?
Scenarios

Consider the following scenarios, and think about how you generally act, what you might be thinking, and how you might be feeling inside.

Scenarios	Words to describe how I act when in this scenario, e.g. 'confident', 'outgoing', 'responsible'	What am I thinking?	What am I feeling?
At school			
With your parents			
With your siblings			
With your friends			
With your girl/boyfriend			
Around adults in authority (e.g. teacher, police officer)			
Alone			

Which one describes the 'real' you? Is there a real you?

_____

_____

Which of these scenarios feels the least like you? For example, it feels as though you're having to pretend to be something you're not, or you feel as though you're playing a role.

_____

_____

Tear Down, Build Up
Outline of a Person

Cognitive Behavioural Techniques(CBT)
CBT Scenarios

Scenarios	What are my immediate thoughts?	What am I feeling?	What are they thinking and feeling?	What might be an alternative explanation for what I think?	What's the evidence to support this thinking?	What do I need?
Your best friend started going out with the boy/girl you like, after you told them about your crush.	She did it on purpose. She's only seeing him to spite me.	Angry, hurt, upset.	She's thinking she's got one over on me. She feels proud of herself.	Maybe she just liked him too and forgot I said I liked him.	She's not usually a mean person and hasn't hurt me like this before.	I need to be understood and heard and for her to accept how I feel. I need her to talk it through with me so we can start over.
Your dad is making you tidy your room when all your friends are going out for the day.						
Your boy/girlfriend is always texting someone and won't let you see their phone.						
Your friend hasn't responded to your text, IM or Facebook message all day.						
Your group of friends keep arguing and spreading rumours about each other, causing drama every day.						

Influences

What are the media?

Resources required: *Large sheets of paper*

Marker pens

Learning objectives: *To encourage young people to recognize that the media are more than just the TV and radio, to consider how the media are accessed through interactive technologies, and to understand how accessing media has changed through the years*

Split the group into two or three smaller groups, and ask them to answer the question, 'What are the media?' The groups should discuss what they think the media are, the types of media, and the means by which we access media. Their answers should be recorded on sheets of paper and used to refer back to.

DISCUSSION POINTS

- *How have the media changed through the years?*

- *What is the purpose of the media?*

- *Has the way we access the media made a difference to the way we absorb information?*

Facilitator notes
- Encourage students to consider as many different types of media as possible, and generate discussion about their use of media. This could provide some useful insights into their behaviours and activities to reflect on in later sessions.

Activity 2.2
Types of Media

Resources required:	*Large sheets of paper*
	Marker pens
Learning objectives:	*To encourage students to identify how much of their day or week is taken up by the media, to understand the role the media play in influencing their perceptions, and to help students identify that what they watch and what they read has positive and negative influences upon them*

Split into small groups, and give each group a large sheet of paper and a different coloured marker pen.

Ask each group to list as many types of media as they can think of in two minutes, for example, TV, magazines, Internet, radio, film.

Request that groups move clockwise (taking their pens with them, but leaving their sheets of paper behind). Now each group is required to look at the types of media listed by the previous group and brainstorm how they use those aspects of the media. Here they will need to make lists of what they watch on TV, what magazines they read, the radio stations they listen to, the social networking sites they visit, and other websites they use.

DISCUSSION POINTS

- *Consider the positive impact these types of media have on*
  - *You?*
  - *On your community?*
  - *On society as a whole?*

- *Do they have any negative impact on*
  - *You?*
  - *On your community?*
  - *On society as a whole?*

- *Does the amount of time we spend watching TV or reading magazines affect how we perceive the media?*

- *Do certain types of media affect us more than others?*

Media Facts

> **Resources required:** *Worksheet 12: Some Facts about the Media – one copy*
>
> *Three sheets of paper for True, False and Don't Know labels*
>
> **Learning objectives:** *To explore the impact the media have on young people, how they view the media, how they think the media influence them, and to identify the positive and negative influences the media can have*

Create some True, False and Don't Know labels (writing one label per sheet of paper) and place them around the room (preferably in a straight line), leaving plenty of space between each one.

Read out the media facts (Worksheet 12: Some Facts about the Media).

Ask the group to decide if they think the fact is true or false and to stand at the corresponding label. They can stand at the 'Don't Know' label (in the middle) if they are unsure.

After they have made their decision, ask them why they think the fact may be true or false before revealing the answer.

DISCUSSION POINTS

After the activity ask the group the following questions:

- *Were you surprised by any of the facts presented to you?*

- *What surprised you the most?*

- *How do you think the media influence young people? (It is worth reiterating here the groups' response to the question, 'Does the amount of time we spend watching TV or reading magazines affect how we perceive the media?', from Activity 2.2. Ask the group if their opinions have changed after hearing the facts about the influences of the media.)*

- *Do the media influence adults as well as young people?*

- *How do you think the media influence adults?*

Facilitator notes

- Encourage as much discussion and debate as possible, and ensure that students are aware that this activity is not a test, and they should not look to others for the answers or copy their friends' decisions.

Reviewing Advertising

Resources required:	*Copies of various magazines*
	Copies of Worksheet 13: Reviewing an Advertisement – one per pair
Learning objectives:	*To enable students to recognize that adverts sell not only a product but also an idea (e.g. a way of life, a value, a need), to encourage students to identify the underlying or subliminal messages that adverts portray and query how that makes us feel, and to consider what we think about ourselves and others as a result of being exposed to these messages*

Randomly pair the group, and provide each pair with a magazine. Ask each pair to look through the magazine and pick an advert that they both find interesting. Using the advert they have chosen, ask them to discuss and answer the questions on Worksheet 13: Reviewing an Advertisement.

DISCUSSION POINTS

- *What attracts our attention to an advert?*

- *What techniques do advertisers use to sell a product? (Record answers on the board to refer back to.)*

- *Are the selling techniques obvious in the adverts that attract us most?*

- *Why do advertisers use certain techniques?*

- *Considering the adverts chosen, what makes us want to buy the product?*

Facilitator notes
- Ensure that the young people understand what the true purpose of an advertisement is (e.g. to make you buy something), but that this can be achieved in many ways, such as buying into an idea or image. For example, lipstick could be the product, but often the idea being sold is beauty – that if you buy this product, you will be beautiful.

Understanding Advertising

Resources required:	*Copies of various magazines*
	Large sheets of paper
	Marker pens
Learning objectives:	*To enable students to identify the common themes running through the adverts in magazines read by young girls and women, and to explore the effect this has on individuals and upon friendship groups*

Recap on Activity 2.4: Reviewing Advertising and ask students to consider the advertisements they had chosen to discuss with their partners. As a group, discuss what persuasion techniques are being used. What would make you buy the product?

Randomly pair the group, and ask them to discuss the following question with their partner:

'If you bought the product, what would you expect?'

In small groups, ask students to divide the large sheet of paper into three columns. In the first column, they should list the products that are often advertised in the magazines they read. In the second column, they should identify any common themes. In the third column, they should list the persuasion techniques that are used by the advertising company. An example is given below.

Product	Theme	Persuasion techniques used
Make-up	Beauty	Celebrity endorsement
Lipstick	Beauty	Attractive models
Hair products	Beauty	Attention from men
		Large fonts
		Colours

DISCUSSION POINTS

- *Which adverts stand out the most to you? Why?*

- *Adverts promote an ideal way of looking or being. How does it feel for those who don't fit that ideal?*

- *Should advertisers be allowed to use these techniques to sell products?*

Facilitator notes

- Encourage discussion about the effects of viewing certain types of adverts, such as low self-esteem, a lack of confidence, questioning identity and idea of self, considering dieting, feeling unhappy with their looks, etc.

- Explore the impact this has upon friendship groups, if friends don't conform with the idea being sold by advertisers.

Impact of Adverts

Resources required:	*Copies of adverts from magazines*
	Sticky tape
	Sticky notes
Learning objectives:	*To enable students to recognize the negative impact that advertising can have on us, to become more aware that an idea is being sold, as well as the product, and to appreciate the impact advertising has upon their thoughts and feelings and how they then impact their thoughts and feelings towards others*

Stick copies of different adverts from different magazines on the walls around the room. Give the students some sticky notes, and ask them to write down:

- The first thought that comes to mind when they see the advert.
- Their first feeling when they see the advert.

They should place each sticky note under the corresponding advert.

Read out the comments made on each sticky note and discuss why it makes us think and feel this way.

DISCUSSION POINTS

- *Are we aware of the effect that advertising has on us?*
- *Are we shocked by the impact that advertising has on us?*
- *Do the thoughts and feelings invoked by adverts make us buy the product?*
- *Could there be long-term effects on individuals who react negatively to advertising? (For example, low self-esteem, developing eating disorders, undergoing plastic surgery.)*
- *Do we view advertising differently knowing the techniques that advertisers use to sell products?*

Facilitator notes
- This activity leads into the activities on airbrushing, where young people start to explore how adverts can be changed to meet the requirements of advertisers.
- Ask the group to identify two adverts from the magazines they read – one selling a product and one selling an idea.
- Ask them to make notes on what is real about the advert and what might not be real.
- Discuss at the next group session.

Airbrushing 1

Resources required: *Copies of images of celebrities and models who have been airbrushed*

Learning objectives: *To support students to recognize where images have been changed, to understand the impact airbrushing has on their thoughts and feelings, and to explore the moral and legal implications of airbrushing images*

Ask the students to compare or play 'spot the difference' with airbrushing images. (You will be able to find images of airbrushed advertisements or pictures of airbrushed celebrities by searching for 'airbrushed images' using an Internet search engine.)

Discuss the students' thoughts about airbrushing and the images they have seen.

DISCUSSION POINTS

- *What shocks us about the images?*

- *Should airbrushing images be illegal?*

- *Should magazines print only proper photos?*

- *Should adverts state that images have been airbrushed?*

- *How does this contribute to how we feel about ourselves and others?*

Facilitator notes

- Encourage students to reflect on their feelings when looking at the images and to explore what needs may be met by buying the product advertised. Are they simply buying a product or trying to meet an emotional need, such as the need for acceptance, approval, acknowledgement, and so on?

Airbrushing 2

Resources required: *Copies of various magazines or images of women from magazines and adverts*

Copies of Worksheet 14: Real or Fake? – one per pair

Learning objectives: *To recognize that images can be changed, and to understand the impact that airbrushed images have on their feelings about themselves and others*

Reiterate to the group that airbrushing is commonplace in advertising and the media, especially in images in adverts and in the magazines we read.

Distribute magazines or images of women from different magazines.

Look at the different images in adverts or images of celebrities and models in a magazine, and discuss what they can see – for example, women who are thin, with a perfect complexion, hair sleek and full of volume, etc.

Remind the group that the image may not be real and that bits of the image may have been changed. In pairs, ask the young people to complete Worksheet 14: Real or Fake?

They should list which parts of the model they think are real and which they think are not real.

DISCUSSION POINTS

• *Was it easy to identify what is real and what might not be real?*

• *Does it make us wary of buying products when we know advertisers change images?*

• *How do we feel when we view images and not know if they have been changed to make them look better?*

Facilitator notes
Young people should be able to:

• identify where images may have been changed

• recognize that adverts and images are selling a product using techniques that are sometimes unethical

• understand how influential images in the media can be.

Social Networking Sites

Resources required: *Ball of yarn*

Large sheets of paper

Pens

Sticky notes

Copy of Worksheet 15: Status Scenarios

Learning objectives: *To encourage young people to recognize that the media are more than just the TV and radio and to consider how the media are accessed through interactive technologies; understanding how accessing media has changed through the years*

Hold a general discussion about who uses social networking sites and which sites they use and what they use it for.

Discuss what are the positives and negatives of using social networking sites. Ask the group to write their answers on sticky notes and stick them onto the large sheets of paper, labelled 'positive' and 'negative' and stuck on the wall in full view.

Seat everyone in a circle. Start with one student who reads a status about someone (Worksheet 15: Status Scenarios), and after reading out the status, throws the ball of yarn to someone (keeping hold of one end of the yarn). The person who catches the yarn should say aloud their 'comment' (which they have to make up – as if they were responding to the actual statement on the social networking site) and throw the ball of yarn to someone else (their 'friend'). Each person should hold on to their end of the yarn as they pass it on, so that a 'spider's web' effect is created. Highlight how the web of yarn creates a visual example of how our status comments connect us to each other. Repeat until everyone has had a go, and the yarn comes back to the facilitator. The facilitator should write all the comments down as they are said.

Review all the comments and discuss:

- How would the person reading the comments feel hearing about it in school?

- How does it affect relationships?

- How far could it spread?

Ask students how many friends they have on their social networking profile. Write down the numbers and add them all up, discussing how many people that one comment could have potentially reached.

DISCUSSION POINTS

- *Can you remove something from your profile?*

- *What impact do statements like this have on other students?*

- *Can you truly remove something from the Internet?*

Facilitator notes

- It is important that the facilitator is familiar with socail networking sites and their purpose and uses for young people.

- Students should be able to recognize their web of friendships online and identify the connections they may have to people they do not know in the real world, highlighting the dangers of strangers potentially viewing anything they post online.

Social Networking

> **Resources required:** *Copies of Worksheet 16: Picture Frame – one per person*
>
> **Learning objectives:** *To help students to recognize they can easily lose control over what they post online, and to identify ways of keeping information private and safe online*

This activity is human bingo, based around social networking.

At the beginning of the session, ask each student to draw five pictures of themselves in the five picture frames, and ask them to write their name on the front. Stress that the pictures don't have to be very wonderful!

Explain that they have to pass one of their pictures to the first person they work with during the lesson. When they receive someone's picture, they should write their name on the back of the picture frame.

Throughout the session, students should pass on a picture to everyone they come into contact with. They can decide whether they want to pass on their own picture or one that's been given to them by someone else.

At the end of the session find out:

- Who has the most pictures of themselves left?

- Who has the least pictures of themselves left?

- Count how many names are on the back of their pictures, and find out who has the highest number.

DISCUSSION POINTS

- *What do the students think was the purpose of that activity?*

- *What happens when we post a photograph on the Internet?*

- *Can pictures be deleted?*

- *What happens when we send a photo by phone?*

- *How can we keep photos and comments we post online private and safe?*

Facilitator notes

- It is important that the facilitator is familiar with social networking sites (used by young people) and site privacy settings to be able to provide guidance and information to young people using such sites. This activity can be used alongside another activity or as a stand-alone session.

Stereotypes

Resources required: *Large sheets of paper*

Pens

Learning objectives: *To identify different stereotypes, to recognize that stereotypes can be inaccurate and unhelpful, and to understand the negative impact of stereotyping individuals*

Split the students into groups, and give each group a large sheet of paper with the word stereotype written in the middle.

Ask each group to write as many types of stereotypes as they can think of. You may wish to provide an example to start, such as 'All girls like to shop' or 'All boys like sports'.

DISCUSSION POINTS

- *What are stereotypes?*

- *Are stereotypes true?*

- *Is it easy to stereotype individuals?*

- *What happens if we stereotype everyone?*

- *What problems may arise if we stereotype people?*

- *Where do stereotypes come from?*

- *Why do we stereotype people?*

- *Are we stereotyped in any way?*

Facilitator notes

Young people will be able to:

- identify stereotypes that exist in their school and community

- explore where stereotypes come from

- understand the impact that stereotypes have on our attitudes and beliefs about others.

Gender Stereotypes

Resources required:	*Worksheet 17: Understanding Gender Stereotypes – one copy*
	Large labels of the numbers 1–5
Learning objectives:	*To encourage students to define gender stereotypes and identify the difference between female and male roles, understanding the impact of gender stereotypes on friendships and social groups, and the effect of gender stereotypes on their thoughts and feelings*

Create large labels of the numbers 1–5, writing one number on each sheet of paper, and spread them out in a line on the floor. Read aloud the statements provided in Worksheet 17: Understanding Gender Stereotypes. Ask students to stand along the line from 1 to 5, where 1 is 'I strongly agree' and 5 is 'I strongly disagree', to indicate how they feel about each statement.

After they have made their decision, discuss their responses to the statements.

DISCUSSION POINTS

- *What are gender stereotypes?*

- *How do we stereotype girls and boys?*

- *Are choices for girls and boys different – in school, in work, in families, in the community?*

- *Who decides how girls should act and how boys should act?*

- *Is it wrong for females to undertake traditionally male roles and for males to undertake traditionally female roles?*

- *Do gender stereotypes affect our thoughts and feelings?*

Facilitator notes

Young people will be able to:

- explore people's attitudes towards traditional gender roles

- explore why gender stereotypes exist

- identify the limitations that gender stereotypes place on both girls and boys

- understand how gender stereotypes impact the choices we make.

Interacting with Others

Resources required:	*Copies of Worksheet 18: How do I Interact with Others? – one per person*
	Copies of Worksheet 19: Scenarios – one per pair
Learning objectives:	*To identify the different ways young people behave in different situations, to recognize the influences of different people and situations on our behaviour, thoughts and feelings, to be aware when our needs and values are not being met in certain circumstances, and to understand the impact that our behaviours have on others in different situations*

Distribute Worksheet 18: How do I Interact with Others? and ask each individual to think about how they behave and communicate with the different people in their lives.

They should consider how they act when they are with family, friends, boys, boyfriends, at school and at home.

Randomly pair the group, and give each pair Worksheet 19: Scenarios. Each person should discuss with their partner how they would behave, speak and act in the given situation and consider why they act in this way (e.g. I feel comfortable in front of my family so I can act silly, or I want my friends to like me so I will act in a way that is acceptable to the group, such as wearing make-up or talking about boys).

DISCUSSION POINTS

- *Has anyone noticed any big differences in the way they act in different circumstances?*

- *Why might this be?*

- *How are we influenced by different people or situations?*

- *Does the way we act in different circumstances meet or conflict with our values and needs?*

- *Look at the positives and negatives to ourselves and others if we behave in ways not in sync with our needs, values and beliefs.*

Facilitator notes
Young people will be able to:

- recognize how they change the way they behave depending on whose company they are in

- explore the reasons why they change their behaviour in different situations

- identify their needs, values and beliefs and how these influence the way they interact with others.

Media Facts
Some Facts about the Media

1. On average, young people aged 14 to 18 watch television for about three hours every day and listen to music or watch music videos for another one to two hours.

TRUE.

Sources: American Academy of Pediatrics, Committee on Public Education (2002) 'Sexuality, contraception, and the media.' *Pediatrics107*, 1, 191–194. Strasburger, V. (1997) 'Sex, drugs, rock 'n roll and the media: Are the media responsible for adolescent behavior?' *Pediatrics 103*, 1, 129–139.

2. Young people aged 13 to 15 ranked their friends as their top source for information on sexuality and sexual health.

FALSE. Young people aged 13 to 15 stated that their top source for information about sexuality and sexual health was entertainment media (TV, magazines, the Internet, etc.).

Source: Kaiser Family Foundation (2001) *Teens and Sex: The Role of Popular TV* (fact sheet). Accessed at www.kff.org/entmedia/loader.cfm?url=/commonspot/security/getfile.cfm&Pageid=13556 on 19 June 2012.

3. Regularly viewing violence online will make you more likely to be violent yourself.

TRUE. Young people who most frequently visited sites depicting real people fighting, shooting or killing were five times more likely to report engaging in assaults, stabbings, robberies and other violent behaviour than were those who never visited violent websites.

Source: Anderson, C.A., Sakamoto, A., Gentile, D.A., Ihori, N., *et al.* (2008) 'Longitudinal effects of violent video games on aggression in Japan and the United States.' *Pediatrics 122*, 5, e1067–e1072.

4. Young people consume an average of six hours of media every day.

FALSE. Young people consume an average of 7 hours and 38 minutes of media every day.

Source: Kaiser Family Foundation (2010) *GENERATION M2: Media in the Lives of 8- to 18-Year-Olds.* Accessed at http://www.kff.org/entmedia/mh012010pkg.cfm on 21 July 2011.

5. Watching sex on TV influences teens to have sex.

TRUE.

Source: Collins, R.L., Elliott, M.N., Berry, S.H., Kanouse, D.E., *et al.* (2004) 'Watching sex on television predicts adolescent initiation of sexual behavior.' *Pediatrics 114*, 3, 280–289.

Reviewing Advertising
Reviewing an Advertisement

Answer the following questions related to an advert you have found in a magazine:

1. What service or product is the advert selling?

_____

_____

2. What idea is the advert selling?

_____

_____

3. What persuasion techniques is this advert using to make you buy?

_____

_____

4. What methods have they used to sell?

_____

_____

5. How does it make you feel to look at the advert?

_____

_____

6. Would you buy the product or service? Why?

_____

_____

Airbrushing 2
Real or Fake?

In the box below, write the name of the magazine the image came from, what product is being sold, and the images used in the advert.

Magazine:	**Product:**
Image:	**Ideas being sold:**

Look at the images being used in the advert/product description, and make a list of the things you think may be real and what may be not be real:

Real:	**Not real:**

What is it about the image that makes you think some things are not real?

_____

_____

Social Networking Sites
Status Scenarios

You can use any of the following scenarios to start the ball of yarn activity, or create your own. Avoid using the name of any person in your group as a scenario example.

- 'Did you see what Georgia was wearing today? How ridiculous did she look…?!'

- 'Do you think I'm afraid of you? You're nothing but a loser and if you can't handle that, it's your problem.'

- 'Kirsten needs to get a life; she is so desperate she would do just about anything to get people to like her.'

- 'Some people would do anything to get a boyfriend, if you know what I mean…'

Social Networking
Picture Frame

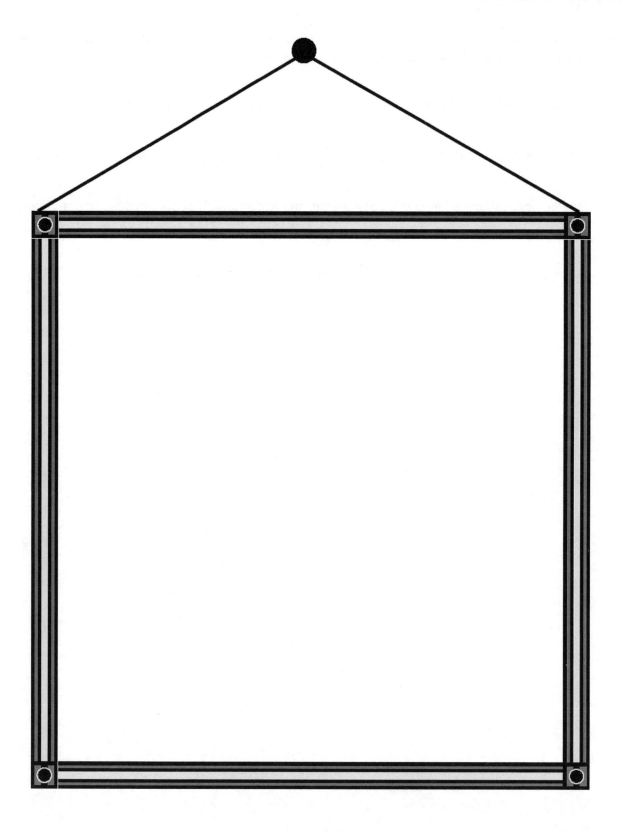

Gender Stereotypes
Understanding Gender Stereotypes

Read the following statements and provide time for the students to choose whether they agree or disagree with them. Discuss their decision after each statement.

1. *Women should be at home cleaning, cooking and looking after the children while men go out to work.*

2. *Men should earn more money than their partners.*

3. *Men can stay at home and look after the children while their wife goes out to work.*

4. *Men make the best chefs.*

5. *Women can do just as good a job as men can in top positions in big companies.*

6. *Women are unable to do the same manual labour jobs as men, such as construction jobs, because they are physically weaker.*

7. *Girls out-perform boys in academic subjects, yet boys out-perform girls in more physical and vocational subjects, such as physical education and woodwork.*

8. *Girls are more creative than boys.*

Interacting with Others
How do I Interact with Others?

For each of the following situations, describe how you would behave and communicate (for example, with my friends I may swear, mess about and show some attitude, but at school I may show respect for teachers and be well mannered).

With friends:	With parents:
Around boys:	**At school:**
With my boyfriend or romantic partner:	**In my community:**
With brothers and sisters:	**Other:**

Interacting with Others
Scenarios

I am at a party	I am standing in a big group of friends	I am in class
I am on Facebook with my best friend	I am shopping with my best friend	I am at home with my family
I am in the park with my friends	I am at a doctor's appointment	I am with my brothers or sisters

Respect, Responsibilities, Relationships

What Happens When?

Resources required: *Large sheets of paper*

Pens

Learning objectives: *To understand that our actions are driven by our thoughts and feelings, which in turn impact our thoughts and feelings of self-worth*

Ask the students to consider things they have done that made them feel good (for example, won a competition or helped a friend). This can be done in small groups with students working together to make a list of actions and activities that promote positive feelings.

Put this list to one side for the time being, and now ask the students to make a list of things they have done that made them feel bad. In their groups, they should list all the actions or situations that evoked negative feelings (for example, drinking, smoking, calling others cruel names, taking things that don't belong to them).

Ask the students to put the two lists side by side to consider and discuss. When looking at the lists, what do we see? The students should notice that the positive lists are things they have done for themselves or to help others, and the negative lists show things usually done to fit in or because they were coaxed into them by others.

DISCUSSION POINTS

- *How do we feel when we undertake actions on the positive list? Does it make us more confident and happy?*

- *How does it feel when we do the things listed on the negative list?*

- *Do we do more of the things on the negative list than we do on the positive list? Why is this?*

Facilitator notes

- By the end of the activity the students should realize that their actions can fuel either positive or negative feelings and thoughts. When asking questions, try to encourage responses that allow the students to reflect upon their actions.

Promoting Self-Respect

> **Resources required:** *Large sheets of paper*
>
> *Lists from Activity 3.1: What Happens When?*
>
> *Pens*
>
> **Learning objectives:** *To highlight that we control our actions and can work at promoting our sense of self*

Refer back to Activity 3.1: What Happens When? and the two lists made by the students.

Taking the list of negative actions, ask students to consider and discuss what happened in the time leading up to their action and behaviour, for example, having an argument with someone, feeling isolated and wanting to fit in, being pressured by peers, failing subjects at school, not being good at sport, etc. List these on the board.

Split the students into small groups or pairs, give each group one of the scenarios on the list, and ask them to come up with a different response to the scenario that will evoke a more positive feeling.

Come back together as a group and discuss the students' responses. Discussing each scenario one at a time, ask the students to discuss the positives and negatives of each response, see if they can add to the response or suggest an alternative.

In a circle, ask each student in turn to consider one thing they could take away from the session that they could implement in the future to prevent undertaking actions that evoke negative responses.

DISCUSSION POINTS

- *Is it easy to say no in certain situations?*

- *Are we always able to think of alternative actions when we are presented with some situations? Or do we need to take our time to think over the consequences of our actions?*

- *Do we always feel in control of our own actions? Why?*

- *What are the consequences of allowing others to control our actions, for example, when others persuade us to do something we would not consider doing at other times?*

Facilitator notes

- This activity is designed to encourage students to look at how they make decisions about their actions. It is important that you emphasize the need to consider all our options before we act.

- Understanding the negative and positive consequences of our actions can help us to make better, more informed choices, and encourages us to consider the impact of our choices on our own thoughts, feelings, values and beliefs.

What are Our Rights?

Resources required:	*Large sheets of paper*
	Pens
Learning objectives:	*To start to explore rights, and to identify what rights apply to them*

As a whole group discuss:

- What are human rights?

- Why are human rights important?

You are not trying to illicit what the students' exact rights are at this point but to get the group to start considering what are human rights – laws that protect us from exploitation and cruelty and legislation to promote equality for everyone. It is also important that they explore the importance of human rights legislation.

Ask the group if they think they are covered by human rights legislation, and establish the group's awareness, understanding and knowledge of the United Nations Convention on the Rights of the Child (UNCRC).

Split the students into small groups, and ask them to write down what they think their rights are. They should consider their rights as:

- young people

- human beings

- girls (or boys).

As a whole group, discuss their answers, drawing out the reasons why they think these rights apply to them and establishing if these rights would also apply to others.

DISCUSSION POINTS

- *Are our rights always recognized by others?*

- *Are there times when our rights have been violated?*

- *Why do you think this might happen?*

- *Are there times when we may have violated other people's rights?*

Facilitator notes

- You may want to familiarize yourself with the UNCRC, which can be found on the UNICEF website at www.unicef.org/crc

What Rights are Important to Me?

Resources required:	*Copies of Worksheet 20: Rights Labels – one per person or one per small group*
Learning objectives:	*To identify what rights are important, and to understand that different rights hold different levels of importance to different people*

Individually or in small groups, cut up and hand out Worksheet 20: Rights Labels. Ask students to think about the rights and consider which they value the most. Ask them to place the rights in order of importance, so the most important right to them will be placed at the top and the least important at the bottom.

After discussion and feedback as a whole group, ask students to look at any differences to the way they ordered the rights that are important to them and how others ordered them.

DISCUSSION POINTS

- *Does everyone have the same rights?*

- *Does everyone value the same rights as you do?*

- *Why do people value different rights?*

- *Does that make them more or less important than you?*

Facilitator notes

- It is important that the students realize that not everyone will value the same rights and they need to be mindful that they may be causing harm to others if they fail to respect the opinions and values of others.

- Discuss with the students how they can manage situations when others do not value the same rights to the same degree.

When Rights are Not Being Met

> **Resources required:** *Images of people in different situations*
>
> **Learning objectives:** *To recognize when people's rights are being violated, to understand that we all have rights that should be respected, and to identify the impact on others when rights are not being respected*

Randomly pair the group and give each pair an image of a person or people whose rights may be violated – you can find images in magazines or books, or by using an online image search. It is a good idea to collect a range of images depicting different people from all walks of life, for example, someone who appears to be living in poverty, someone in a war zone, a child being bullied. Alternatively, if you have extra time and the use of computers with Internet access, you can ask the students to conduct an online search for images themselves.

Ask the students to consider:

- What is happening in the picture?

- What human rights do they think are being violated?

- What impact does this violation have upon the individual, family, community and society as a whole?

Ask each pair to feed back their observations to the rest of the group.

Following on from this exercise, begin to look at the rights that may not be being met in our own friendship groups, schools and communities. Why do our rights get violated, and who does it affect? Ask the group to consider what impact this has upon their relationships with others.

DISCUSSION POINTS

- *How does it make us feel to see others mistreated and having their rights violated?*

- *What were our initial thoughts when we saw the pictures?*

- *Do we feel the same way when considering the rights violated within our friendship groups, schools and communities? Why?*

Facilitator notes

- This exercise is designed to encourage the group to begin to acknowledge that breaching someone's rights does not always happen in less developed countries or on a national level, but can happen in our own schools, communities and friendships.

- It is important the students begin to realize that *they* can violate other people's rights and to understand the impact this can have upon their friendships with others.

Who's Responsible?

Resources required:	*Copies of Worksheet 21: Scenarios – one per person*
Learning objectives:	*To understand our personal responsibility, and to identify who is responsible for our thoughts, feelings and behaviours*

Give each individual a copy of Worksheet 21: Scenarios. Ask the students to read each scenario and consider if they would have any responsibility in the given situation, and if so to consider the level of responsibility they have.

1 on the scale equates to no personal responsibility, and 10 equates to having full personal responsibility in this situation.

Discuss their answers, and explore the reasons behind their answers.

Draw the thoughts, feelings, behaviour triangle on the board, and discuss how our thoughts influence our feelings, which in turn influence our behaviour, providing an example as necessary.

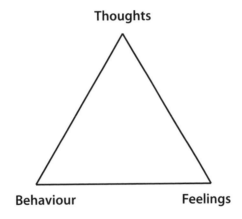

Discuss – who is responsible for our thoughts? Our feelings? Our behaviours?

DISCUSSION POINTS

- *Do we attribute our feelings and behaviours to the actions of others?*

- *Why do we sometimes blame others for the way we feel, think and behave?*

- *Are we in control of our thoughts, feelings and behaviours?*

Facilitator notes
- Encourage the students to start thinking about how others can affect their thoughts, feelings and behaviours.

- Consider ways they can begin to control their own thoughts, feelings and behaviour, using positive thinking, affirmations and taking time to evaluate situations and things that are said.

Locus of Control

> **Resources required:** *Copies of Worksheet 22: Scenarios – one per person*
>
> **Learning objectives:** *To understand external and internal locus of control, and to identify what is within and what is outside of an individual's control*

Read aloud the explanations of an internal and external locus of control (Worksheet 22: Scenarios). Ask the group if they can think of examples of internal and external locus of control, and record on the board, answers in columns.

Distribute copies of Worksheet 22: Scenarios and ask the students to complete it individually. As a group, discuss the answers and reasons behind why they think each is internal or external locus of control.

DISCUSSION POINTS

- *Can we control everything that happens in our lives?*

- *What happens if we don't feel in control? How do we feel?*

- *What do we think? How do we behave?*

- *Is there anything we could we do if we have no control or little control over a situation? What could we do? (You could use this as an additional activity and ask small groups to create solution boards to identify things they could do to make them feel like they have power in situations where they have no control or little control. These could include discussing the problem with someone they trust or looking for information that can help those involved.)*

Facilitator notes

- Often young people feel that they have to be control of everything, and when they are unable to control certain situations, such as parental divorce or someone getting ill, they struggle to manage in that situation.

- It is important that the students know they are unable to control everything in their lives, and at some point they will encounter situations that they will be unable to change.

- Providing the students with a valid understanding of this is important. Ensure you look at practical examples of what they can do to help them feel they can at least take action to help the situation.

'I am Responsible and in Control'

Resources required:	*Worksheet 23: Level of Responsibility Scenarios – one copy*
	Three large sheets of paper for the responsibility labels
Learning objectives:	*To understand that individuals are fully responsible for their actions, to identify situations when they may be influenced by others, understanding that they can control their own actions*

In preparation for this activity you will need to create three 'responsibility labels', each one written on a large sheet of paper.

Across the length of the room, place the responsibility labels at equal distances from each other. At one end of the room, place a label that reads 'I am totally responsible for my actions.' At the other end, place a label that reads 'I am not responsible for my actions.' In the middle, place a label that reads 'I am only partly responsible for my actions.'

Read aloud the scenarios (e.g. 'My friend passed me the bottle of alcohol and told me to drink some, so I did) in Worksheet 23: Level of Responsibility Scenarios. Ask students to consider if they think they are responsible for their actions, and to stand by the label they think most applies to them. Remind them that this is a personal answer and they should stand where they believe their level of responsibility lies and not where others stand.

Discuss their answers and the reasons why they believe they are or are not responsible for their actions.

DISCUSSION POINTS

- *What happens when we don't take responsibility for our actions with our friends?*

- *How often do we do things based on what others have said they have done?*

- *How do we feel when we do things just because others have done them?*

- *What do we think? How do we then behave?*

Facilitator notes

- Young people often partake in activities because their friends persuade them to do it, or tell them they have done it and it was fun, or pressure them into doing something to fit into the group.

- It is important to understand that this often leads to internal and external conflicts, and can have damaging consequences for health, well-being, academic results and social accomplishments.

- Encourage the students to identify ways they can resist pressure and avoid situations that can be harmful to them as individuals.

- It is important to emphasize friendship traits that encourage individuality and support each person's decision not to partake in social activities they aren't interested in. This will encourage the young people to identify those friendships that can be destructive and negative.

The Problem with Rumours

Resources required:	*Bowl of water*
	Food colouring
Learning objectives:	*To understand the impact of rumours on friendships, individuals and others, and to identify why rumours are started and why young people use rumour spreading to hurt others, and to understand our responsibilities when we hear a rumour*

Using a bowl of water, discuss how our friendship group can be influenced by rumours and gossip. Ask the group to invent a rumour, and add a drop of food colouring to the water to represent the rumour being spread around a school.

Ask the group if a rumour stays the same as it is being spread from one person to the next or whether it changes in any way. Discuss ideas for how rumours spread, continuing to add drops of food colouring to the water to represent each time the rumour is spread to another person.

Discuss how muddied and discoloured the water becomes the more and more people hear the rumour and add to it, extending the problem.

DISCUSSION POINTS

- *Are rumours based on fact?*

- *Why do we think rumours start? Do we enjoy gossip?*

- *Why do rumours continue to spread and grow?*

- *What are we thinking and feeling when we start rumours?*

- *What do you think the subject of the rumour or gossip is thinking and feeling?*

- *Does the message in a rumour go away once people stop spreading them?*

- *What are our responsibilities to our friends?*

Facilitator notes

- Rumours are used to destroy reputations and hurt an individual.

- Rumours have an immediate impact because of the nature of what is being said, which can leave young people feeling isolated and ridiculed by their peers, regardless of whether they believe the rumour or not.

- It is important that the students understand the short- and long-term effects of rumours.

What is Respect?

Resources required: *Images of people in different professions*

Ball of string

Plastic clothes pegs

Learning objectives: *To understand what respect is, to create a personal definition of respect, and to understand that respect means different things to different people*

Discuss as a whole group what 'respect' is and what respect means to us individually. Highlight that respect means different things to different people.

Split the group into pairs, and ask each pair to look at a set of images depicting people in different professions. You can use images from magazines, books or an online search. It is important to find a range of images, for example, a factory worker, police officer, teacher, cleaner, fire fighter, office worker, etc. Create a 'washing line' with the ball of string. Using the images of people in different roles, ask each pair to discuss and peg each image on the 'washing line' in order of the person they would show the most respect down to the person they would show least respect to. Discuss the reasons why students show different people different levels of respect.

Repeat the activity, and ask each pair to consider who they would expect respect from, ordering the images from who they would want to respect them the most, down to who they expect the least respect from. Discuss why they require or expect more respect from some people over others.

DISCUSSION POINTS

- *Why is respect important?*

- *Do we use the term 'respect' too loosely?*

- *Do we mistake what respect means to different people?*

- *What happens if we disrespect others? Or others disrespect us?*

- *How do we feel when others fail to show us respect? What do we think? How do we behave?*

- *Do people have to earn respect?*

Facilitator notes

- Respect is a term often used by young people but is not really understood. By breaking down what respect means to them, for example, being listened to, others portraying good manners towards them, being made to feel their views and opinions count, you begin to unpick what this all-encompassing term means on an individual level.

- Once young people know what respect means to them, they can understand when someone is disrespecting them and can feel confident to communicate this to others. It is important to discuss what they should do in situations when they feel disrespected. Helpful actions could include positive thinking, or telling the other person how they have made them feel.

What is Friendship?

Resources required: *Copies of Worksheet 24: Friendship Pyramid – one per pair*

Learning objectives: *To understand what friendship is, to identify the traits required in our friends, and to understand that friendships are based on respect and individuality*

Before commencing this activity, make copies of Worksheet 24: Friendship Pyramid, cut up the statements, so each group can have a copy of all the traits.

Randomly split the group into pairs. Give each pair a set of friendship traits (Worksheet 24: Friendship Pyramid). Explain to the group that each pair will discuss what traits they expect from friends and what are the most important traits for friends to have. Ask each pair of students to make a pyramid, with the one most important trait they want in their friends at the top of the pyramid, then the next two placed below, then the next three and so on, to the five least important traits at the bottom.

As a whole group, discuss what traits the students consider to be important, and ask the group to reflect on their own friendships and consider if their friends share the top traits they consider to be important.

DISCUSSION POINTS

- *Do we choose our friends based on the traits we consider important in our friendships?*

- *What happens if our friends do not have the traits we consider important?*

- *Are there reasons why we would choose friends that do not possess the traits we consider important?*

- *Do friendships last if the traits that we consider important are not present?*

- *Is respect in friendships important?*

Facilitator notes

- Young people often choose friendships based on social status, and as such, their friends do not always have the traits they consider important to them. Often, friends do not have common interests, and trust between friends does not exist.

- It is important that the students recognize that their friendships are often destructive because they are based on social status, fear or convenience, rather than based upon support or encouragement.

- You can repeat this activity for romantic relationships using the same traits as in Worksheet 24. Ask the group, in their pairs, to discuss the traits they consider important in a romantic relationship. Discuss any differences and similarities, and ask the group to consider why they think there are differences and similarities from the friendship activity. Should the traits we look for in romantic relationships differ from the traits we look for in our friends?

Respecting 'Me' 1

Resources required:	*Pictures of young women*
Learning objectives:	*To understand the concept of respecting 'me', to identify when someone may not be respecting themselves, to understand the impact that a lack of respect for oneself can have on others, and to build an appreciation that respect means different things to different people*

Discuss with the group what they think self-respect means. Record answers on the board so they are visible throughout the duration of the activity.

Distribute a set of images of young women to the group – you can find images in magazines, or from an online search. It is important to find a wide range of images that would encourage debate about whether the subjects of the image respect themselves or not. For example, you could find images of young women drinking alcohol, smoking, partaking in sports, studying or bullying others.

Working in small groups, ask students to consider which of the young women may be confident and have high self-esteem. Ask them to put the images into two columns: one column for the young women they think have respect for themselves, are confident and have high self-esteem, and the second column for the young women they believe have a lack of respect for themselves.

As a group, discuss their decisions to put each image into each column.

DISCUSSION POINTS

- *Are these people trying to meet their needs in some way?*

- *What needs might they be trying to meet?*

- *Is there a better way to meet these needs and to show themselves more respect?*

- *Have we ever done anything that conflicts with our values and shows a lack of respect for ourselves?*

- *Do we take part in activities just to fit in? Does this show a lack of respect for ourselves? What could we do instead?*

Facilitator notes

- Be mindful to point out that just because a young woman is smoking or has a tattoo, it doesn't necessarily mean that she does not respect herself.

- Remind the students that respect means different things to different people, and at times, young women may be trying to fulfil a need by partaking in such activities which may be deemed as disrespectful.

Respecting 'Me' 2

Resources required: *Copies of Worksheet 25: Respect Diary – one per person*

Learning objectives: *To understand the concept of respecting 'me', to identify when someone may not be respecting themselves, to understand the impact a lack of respect for oneself can have on others, and to build an appreciation that respect means different things to different people*

As an extension to Activity 3.12: Respecting 'Me' 1, distribute individual copies of Worksheet 25: Respect Diary. Ask the group to keep a diary over a specified period of time, anything from one week to one month. Each day the students should reflect on activities they have been involved in, things they have done, clothes they have worn, conversations they have had and places they have visited.

- Ask the students to log what they were thinking, what they were feeling and how they were behaving.

- Ask them to consider and record if they felt they were showing themselves respect during that period of time and if they were showing respect for others.

- In the final column, the students should start to consider what they could have done differently to ensure they acted in a way that reflected their values and showed respect to themselves and others.

Facilitator notes

- This is a personal diary log and it should be pointed out to the students that it will be a confidential log and doesn't have to be shared with other young people in the group.

- You may want to arrange to meet each person individually to reflect on the outcomes of the diary log and to reassure them that it is normal to go through a period where we try to fit in at the expense of our own self-respect.

- It is important to point out that this exercise is meant to encourage young people to think about their actions before they partake in activities and to learn to identify alternatives to ensure more positive outcomes for themselves and others.

Respecting 'Me' 3

Resources required: *Talking piece*

Learning objectives: *To understand the concept of respecting 'me', to identify when someone may not be respecting themselves, to understand the impact a lack of respect for oneself can have on others, and to build an appreciation that respect means different things to different people*

Sit in a circle and pass around a talking piece (e.g. an object, such as a ball, that indicates that the person holding the object can talk while the others listen. You may need to explain the role of the talking piece to groups who are not familiar with the process). Ask each person to consider and answer the following: 'How did I show respect for myself and others today in this session?'

As the group is discussing respect, ensure that respect is being modelled throughout the activity. Thus, everyone should be respectful and listen to what others have to say and respect confidentiality in the group.

Facilitator notes

- As the facilitator, it is important that you model what is expected from the group. Showing respect and partaking in the activity are both essential.

- You should never ask the group to do something that you are not willing to do yourself.

- Modelling the behaviour you want to see from the group will enhance their learning and help to foster an environment of mutual respect and understanding.

- You can choose to answer first and allow the group to follow on with their answers – which will be useful if the group struggles with the activity – or you can choose to wait to answer at the end of the activity.

Passive/Assertive/Aggressive

Resources required:	*Copies of Worksheet 26: Am I Passive, Assertive or Aggressive? – one per pair of students*
Learning objectives:	*To understand the differences between passive, assertive, and aggressive behaviours, to identify when they are being aggressive or passive, to be aware of the affect this has on others, and to be able to be assertive in their interactions with others*

In pairs, complete Worksheet 26: Am I Passive, Assertive or Aggressive.

Ask the group to consider if they can tell if someone is either aggressive or passive. How do they know if someone is aggressive or passive? How do these people make them feel? How do they behave around people who are aggressive or passive? Why do we behave in this way?

As a group, discuss what it means to be assertive, and record the answers on the board.

DISCUSSION POINTS

- *Does our behaviour affect the way others react to us?*

- *Are we aware of our tone of voice or body language when we are interacting with others?*

- *Do we mostly interact with others in an aggressive or passive manner?*

- *How do others react to us?*

- *Is it easy to be assertive?*

- *How do we learn assertiveness?*

- *How do we interact with people who are assertive?*

Continue the activity with a role play session. In pairs, assign each person a letter A or B. Give Person A one of the following statements which they must say to Person B, first, in a passive manner and then in an aggressive manner, or ask students to create their own statements if they prefer. Person B must respond assertively.

Reverse roles so Person A is given the opportunity to practise being assertive.

Statements:

"You are so mean, I can't believe you would say that to me!"

"Why are you doing this to me?"

"Why don't you want to be my friend anymore?"

"Why did you tell Jane those lies about me?"

As a whole group, discuss how each person felt when their statements were responded to in an assertive manner. How did they feel when they were being assertive? What were they thinking and feeling?

Facilitator notes

- Conflict often occurs when young people interact with others aggressively or passively. Teaching young people to be assertive allows them to avoid situations and partaking in activities that may cause them harm and conflict with their values and beliefs.

What Would I Expect?

Resources required: *Copies of Worksheet 27: Scenarios – one per small group*

Learning objectives: *To explore what is acceptable or unacceptable in relationships, and to understand limitations and expectations in relationships*

Split the group into small groups. Give each group a copy of Worksheet 27: Scenarios and ask them to decide if the scenarios are acceptable or unacceptable.

Discuss the results as a whole group, and share thoughts about our expectations.

DISCUSSION POINTS

- *What if our expectations aren't met? (For example, our partner doesn't treat us nicely.)*

- *How do we communicate our expectations to others, including our friends and family, about how we want to be treated?*

Facilitator notes

- This activity is aimed at encouraging young people to start exploring what is acceptable behaviour from a romantic partner. It is important that the students discuss the importance of establishing firm boundaries in romantic and platonic relationships to ensure they remain safe and in control.

- Establishing boundaries and communicating expectations will enable relationships to grow and flourish without conflicts arising.

What Rights are Important to Me?
Rights Labels

To be free to be myself	To feel safe	To be able to go to school
To be healthy	To live with my parents	To practise a religion of my choice
To join groups and organizations of my choice, provided I do not stop others enjoying their human rights	To be able to have things I say and do kept private if I ask for confidentiality	To have my opinions count when adults are making decisions that affect me
To be able to share information with others	To be able to access information held about me	To be free from abuse and neglect
To be able to access medical help as I need it	To be able to have enough food and water to survive	To be able to learn about my own culture and beliefs at school and to be able to use my first language
To be able to play and enjoy a variety of activities	To know what my rights are	To be respected by others

Who's Responsible?
Scenarios

Consider the following scenarios, and decide if you would have any responsibility in the given situation. On a scale of 1 to 10, where 1 is 'I have no responsibility' and 10 is 'I have full responsibility', determine your level of responsibility in the situations by circling a number.

Scenario 1

Your parents ask you to look after your younger brother while they go and pick your grandmother up from the hospital. While they are gone, you leave your brother to play in your father's home office. He ruins a number of important documents. Are you responsible for the ruined documents?

1	2	3	4	5	6	7	8	9	10

Scenario 2

You are out with your friends at the local park. You and one of your friends have managed to purchase some alcohol. You pass the alcohol around the group to share. One of your friends gets really drunk and starts to feel ill. The next morning, you are told your friend was taken to hospital. Are you responsible for your friend getting drunk?

1	2	3	4	5	6	7	8	9	10

Scenario 3

You, along with others, make fun of your friend because she has never kissed a boy. Your friend is upset by the comments and the jokes made at her expense. Are you responsible for making your friend upset?

1	2	3	4	5	6	7	8	9	10

Scenario 4

You are tired with your friends constantly making fun of the clothes you wear. Your parents refuse to buy you new clothes because they do not see anything wrong with the ones you are wearing. The next time you are out shopping, you decide to steal a few new tops from your favourite clothes store. Are you responsible for your actions?

1	2	3	4	5	6	7	8	9	10

Locus of Control
Scenarios

There are two ways of looking at the things that happen in your life: either they just happen to you and you have no control over them, or they are something that you can influence and change. You can either say:

- 'It's my fault' / 'It's within my control' (internal locus of control)

    or

- 'It's someone else's fault' / 'I can't change it' (external locus of control)

Internal locus of control means that you can take pride in any successes you achieve as they are down to you, but at the same time, you take responsibility for any failures in your life because they are equally your responsibility.

External locus of control means that you are unable to accept responsibility for your own lack of effort or control; you blame bad things that happen on someone else.

Read the following scenarios and decide whether you control the situation or others are in control, by circling the appropriate response:

1. I got a good grade in science; all the studying I have been doing has really helped.

    I am in control   I have no control

2. I was late for school because my sister refused to get dressed this morning.

    I am in control   I have no control

3. I failed my history test because my teacher doesn't like me.

    I am in control   I have no control

4. I wasn't allowed to go to the party with my friends because I misbehaved at home.

    I am in control   I have no control

5. The people I hang around with made me bully younger children.

    I am in control   I have no control

6. The whole class was given detention because one person misbehaved during the lesson.

    I am in control   I have no control

7. The people I spend time with made me smoke.

    I am in control   I have no control

'I am Responsible and in Control'
Level of Responsibility Scenarios

Read the following scenarios, and ask students to consider if they think they are responsible for their actions and to stand by the card they think most applies to them.

1. My friend passed me the bottle of alcohol and told me to drink some, so I did.

2. I found someone else's phone in my bag; I was later told that a friend hid it there as a joke.

3. I wouldn't go on a date with Ben because my friends would laugh at me, even though I really like him.

4. Jodie pushed me into Gemma on purpose.

5. I started smoking because all the cool people smoke.

6. I told my boyfriend I wasn't comfortable with doing anything more than kissing and told him I wouldn't do more just because my friends tell me *they* have.

7. I went on a date with Tom because he is the best looking boy in school, and I knew it would make my friends jealous.

8. I refused to skip class with the other girls, even though I knew they would talk about me behind my back.

What is Friendship?
Friendship Pyramid

Someone my friends like being with too

Someone I am proud of

Doesn't show off to others

Is good fun to be with

Someone who is trustworthy

Listens to what I have to say

Shares their feelings with me

Is good looking

Is intelligent

Does not spread rumours and gossip behind my back

Makes an effort to be clean and tidy

Likes the same stuff as me

Chooses to spend time with me

Asks me about what I think

Has lots of friends

Respecting 'Me' 2
Respect Diary

Date	What I did	What I was thinking	How I was feeling	Was I respecting myself and others?	What I could have done differently

Passive/Assertive/Aggressive
Am I Passive, Assertive or Aggressive?

This is me…	Am I passive, assertive or aggressive?
I speak really loudly; most of the time I shout at others.	
I walk around with my shoulders slouched and my face down.	
If I am upset, I will communicate my distress clearly and calmly. I will start my sentences with 'I feel upset because…'	
Others sometimes turn the other way when they see me coming, and my friends do what I say to avoid being threatened.	
People enjoy being friends with me because I take time to listen and communicate my feelings clearly.	
People often make fun of me because I find it difficult to stand up for myself.	
I often ridicule and threaten others for fun.	
I speak clearly and confidently, and people can always hear what I say.	
I often mumble and get embarrassed when I talk; others find it difficult to hear me.	

What Would I Expect?
Scenarios

Read the following scenarios about how a girlfriend or boyfriend might treat their partner when in a relationship, and consider whether you feel the behaviour is acceptable or unacceptable, or if it depends on the situation, by circling the appropriate answer.

Remember, there are no right or wrong answers – just your opinion. Consider yourself in that situation, and decide how you would feel: would you expect your partner to treat you that way?

1. Texting me all the time, even if I don't respond to the last message.
   Acceptable   Unacceptable   Depends on situation

2. Telling me I am overweight or need to exercise more.
   Acceptable   Unacceptable   Depends on situation

3. Putting their arm around me when we're out in public.
   Acceptable   Unacceptable   Depends on situation

4. Always correcting me and interrupting what I say.
   Acceptable   Unacceptable   Depends on situation

5. Hitting me if I cheat on them.
   Acceptable   Unacceptable   Depends on situation

6. Making me feel guilty for not wanting to be physically intimate (e.g. have sex).
   Acceptable   Unacceptable   Depends on situation

7. Buying me gifts and presents.
   Acceptable   Unacceptable   Depends on situation

8. Asking where I am going or where I've been.
   Acceptable   Unacceptable   Depends on situation

Theme 4

Managing Relationships

Concentric Circles

Resources required: *Copies of Worksheet 28: Concentric Circles in My Life – one per person*

Learning objectives: *To begin to explore the relationships we have with others*

Ask the students to complete Worksheet 28: Concentric Circles in My life individually. Students will need to consider all of the different people in their life, from close loved ones to acquaintances, exploring the concept of what a 'relationship' is and what it means to be in a relationship with someone.

Students should write the names or initials of any people they have a relationship with in the corresponding circle – from close relationships in the inner circle to distant acquaintances in the outer circle.

DISCUSSION POINTS

- *How many people could you think of to write in the circles?*

- *How would it feel to not have any names to write in the inner circles, such as someone who is isolated and bullied at school?*

- *What are our expectations of the people in our circles?*

- *Do our expectations change or increase for those who are closest to us?*

- *How does that affect our relationships with those people?*

Facilitator notes
- You may wish to spend some time discussing what a relationship is and how a friendship or connection with an acquaintance is still a relationship.

Friendship Agree/Disagree

Resources required:	*Worksheet 29: Statements – one copy*
	Three sheets of paper
Learning objective:	*To begin to explore the concept of friendship*

Write the words 'Agree', 'Disagree' and 'Don't know' on three separate pieces of paper and spread them across the floor at equal distances. The facilitator should read the Friendship Agree/Disagree Statements on Worksheet 29 aloud, and students should decide whether they agree or disagree with the statements, or if they don't know, by voting with their feet. Explain the rules of the agree/disagree game. Stress the importance of there being no right or wrong answer and that students should make their own decisions, rather than following their friends.

After each statement, discuss why students agree or disagree and generate discussion based on students' responses.

DISCUSSION POINTS

- *Discuss the effects of expecting too much of our friends.*

- *Explore whether we expect one person or others to meet our needs.*

Friends or Not?

Resources required: *Images of friends – one set per small group*

Learning objectives: *To explore how we choose our friends, and to understand why*

Split the students into small groups, preferably mixing up groups of friends. Give each group a copy of a selection of images of friends – you can find these in magazines, or through an online image search. Ensure that you have a good range and selection of images, including different types of young people represented, from stereotypical images of studious young people or 'Queen Bee' popular girls, to young people from a wide range of religious and cultural backgrounds.

Students should work together to split the images into three categories – people they would be friends with, or be friendly to, or neither. Students need to consider why they are placing the people in each category.

DISCUSSION POINTS

- *How do we choose our friends?*

- *What draws us to some people over others?*

- *Do we judge people by their appearance?*

- *What are the most important qualities for a friend to have?*

- *What is the difference between being friends and being friendly?*

Breaking and Strengthening Friendships

Resources required: *A long length of string or ribbon*

Scissors

Learning objectives: *To understand how friendships can be broken and strengthened*

Gather the students into a circle and ask everyone to hold the string or ribbon, allowing plenty of slack, so that a loose circle of string or ribbon is created.

Stand in the middle of the circle with the scissors and ask each student to name one thing that can break a friendship. As they do, cut the string. Repeat until each person has named something.

Repeat the exercise, this time asking students to name something they can do to strengthen friendships. As students state what they can do to strengthen their friendships, have them tie their string to the person's next to them, so that the circle is re-created.

DISCUSSION POINTS

- *Are we more likely to strengthen or break friendships?*

- *Are friendships healed when we make amends? (Draw the students' attention to how the circle of string was re-created but wasn't the same.)*

Relationship Skills

Split the students into small groups, and give each group a copy of Worksheet 30: Friendship Scenarios. Give each group time to discuss the scenarios and to list as many solutions to the problems as they can think of on a large sheet of paper.

Gather the groups back together and discuss the solutions they identified for the scenarios. Tack the papers to the wall or board, and discuss any similarities or overlaps in the solutions, identifying any common themes.

Ask students to identify what skills they need to use or what attributes would help them in these scenarios, listing them on the board or on paper (e.g. listening skills, patience, respect, being humble, speaking assertively, displaying confidence).

Time allowing, put students into pairs, and ask them to act out one or more of the scenarios, first without using the solutions they identified and then practising the skills and attributes that will help them to build or maintain the relationship.

DISCUSSION POINTS

- *What stops us sometimes from using these skills or attributes, such as taking the time to listen to our friend's point of view?*

- *What is the consequence of not using these relationship skills?*

- *What is the one relationship skill you would benefit from practising more often?*

Best Friends Forever (BFF)

Resources required:	*Copies of Worksheet 31: The BFF Quiz – one per person*
Learning objectives:	*To encourage students to consider their own values and beliefs about friendship, including their definition and expectations of a friend, and their own friendship persona*

Hand out a copy of Worksheet 31: The BFF Quiz to each student and give them at least ten minutes or more to complete. Students should be encouraged to take their time and to consider their responses carefully. This is not a test and no one will know their answers.

The BFF Quiz encourages students to explore themes, such as how they view their friends, what a best friend means to them, peer pressure, and to consider how well they treat their friends.

When complete, ask students for their general feedback, without pushing anyone to disclose any specific answers unless they feel comfortable to do so.

DISCUSSION POINTS

- *Was anyone surprised by their results?*

- *Did the questions make you think about your friends and yourself as a friend a little more?*

Cliques

Resources required: *Copies of Worksheet 32: Clique Scenarios – cut up into cards and placed in a bowl*

Learning objectives: *To understand the difference between a healthy and unhealthy group of friends, and to explore the behaviours of cliques*

Discuss what is meant by the term 'clique' and what a clique might look like or behave like, noting any words or phrases on the board (for example, pushing people out, bullying, not allowing others to join in).

Discuss what the opposite of a clique might look and feel like – an inclusive circle of friends where people feel welcomed and feel as though they belong. Draw on students' experiences of both inclusive circles and cliques, including any examples they have seen on TV or in films. The movie *Mean Girls* is a good example of how a group of friends can become a negative clique.

Ask the students to stand in a large circle, and ask three people to volunteer to stand in a smaller circle inside. Explain to students that this is the 'clique', while the outer circle is the circle of belonging.

Nominate a person to go first and to randomly take one of the scenarios (from Worksheet 32) from the bowl and read it aloud. The student should decide whether the scenario describes cliquish behaviour, in which case they should join the circle in the middle, or inclusive, friendly behaviour, in which case they should stay in the outer circle. Repeat until everyone has read a scenario and the two circles are complete.

DISCUSSION POINTS

- *How does it feel to be standing in the clique (for those in the belonging circle)?*

- *How does it feel to see those people in the clique and to be separate from it (for those in the outer circle)?*

- *Would anyone choose to react differently to their scenario they read out?*

- *Does anyone recognize that they have been a part of a clique? How does that feel now, seeing the people who are part of a circle of belonging?*

- *How does it feel to belong to something, like a circle of friends?*

The Drama Triangle

Resources required: *Worksheet 33: The Drama Triangle – one per person*

Learning objectives: *To develop awareness of the dynamic created by conflict in relationships, to enhance students' understanding of the roles they might play, and to appreciate why*

Discuss as a whole group what can happen when friendships go wrong, highlighting the three roles that can occur – victim, rescuer and perpetrator. Ensure that students understand and are aware of what the three terms mean, exploring how each person may feel and act.

Explore the example of a friendship group where two people have an argument and one ends up hitting the other, with the third friend stuck in the middle.

DISCUSSION POINTS

- *Which person is the victim? The rescuer? The perpetrator?*

- *How might each person feel?*

- *What might each person do next?*

- *Has anyone ever experienced a situation like this?*

- *Did anyone ever start out in one role (e.g. the victim of a friendship fallout) and somehow slip into another role (e.g. becoming the perpetrator by retaliating and doing something back)?*

Highlight to students how the drama triangle describes the three roles and how they can swap and change frequently, so that the victim might become the perpetrator, or the rescuer might become the victim – this can happen in bullying situations also. By swapping roles, the 'drama' of friendship groups is constantly fuelled so that friendships never feel healthy, safe and fun.

Give each student a copy of Worksheet 33: The Drama Triangle, and ask them to complete it individually.

DISCUSSION POINTS

- *Did anyone learn anything about themselves by completing this worksheet (that they would like to share)?*

- *What drama drivers did you identify that happen in your friendship group?*

- *Is there a role that you recognize which describes you or someone you know the most?*

- *What strategies did you identify for escaping the drama triangle?*

Circles of Conflict

> **Resources required:** *Small bottle of perfume or scent, preferably very floral or strong smelling*
>
> **Learning objective:** *To build students' awareness of how conflict can spread*

Discuss what the term 'conflict' means, and write examples of conflict on the board, from minor disputes between friends or family to full-scale war – all of which are examples of conflict.

Ask the students to identify some examples of conflicts that have occurred within their friendship groups, without naming anyone's name or embarrassing others. Highlight how these conflicts can spread – an argument between two people can quickly include a whole friendship group when others get involved or take sides.

Ask students to stand up and position themselves around the room. Without other students looking (preferably before the activity starts), ask two students to be secret helpers and spray a small amount of perfume or scent onto their hand (depending on whether they are right or left handed). You should decide whether it is appropriate for you to be involved in this activity – if yes, then discreetly spray some scent onto your hand also.

Instruct students that they must move around the room and shake hands with anyone they have ever had a conflict with or anyone whose conflict they have heard about (e.g. you hear about a friend of a friend having a fight with someone). Give students only two minutes to do this, so they move quickly around the room. The secret helpers can initiate the handshaking and encourage anyone who is reluctant.

Once complete, ask students what they notice about their hands. Everyone in the room should have the same perfume on their hand that has been spread from the two initial people.

DISCUSSION POINTS

- *How did the perfume spread itself around the room?*

- *How does conflict spread itself around a friendship group, class or even a whole school?*

- *What can we do to avoid spreading conflict and to stop it before it starts?*

Facilitator notes

- Highlight to students that in this instance we were demonstrating how conflict and bad feeling can quickly spread, but good feeling and acts of friendship and kindness can just as easily spread – except the results are quite different! Just as we need to make an effort not to spread conflict, we need to make an effort to spread positive energy and good feeling.

Tipping the Scales

Resources required:	*One or more sets of weighing scales (ideally)*
	Small marbles or similar – enough for at least ten per small group
Learning objectives:	*To develop students' awareness of the balance of friendships and the impact of their behaviour*

Split the students into small groups or pairs, depending on how many sets of scales and marbles you have. Ask students to consider:

- Positive friendship actions they have taken this week
- Negative friendship actions they have taken this week

Discuss examples of each, such as asking someone to sit with you, keeping a secret for a friend; spreading a rumour about someone, or calling them a name.

For each positive and negative action, students should place a marble on the scale – one side for positive, the other for negative to 'weigh up' their actions. Give students around five minutes to do this and then swap over so that everyone gets a chance to go.

DISCUSSION POINTS

- *Did you have more positive marbles or negative marbles?*
- *How does it feel to think about your actions this week and see it in front of you?*
- *Is there anything you would do differently now?*
- *Did anyone have about the same number of positive and negative marbles?*
- *What is the impact of this? Does the good cancel out the bad, or do people still get affected by what we do?*
- *How do our negative marbles leave us and others feeling?*

Facilitator notes
- It may be difficult to find enough scales for all the students to have a go, so simply using the marbles will work for this activity, although some of the visual effect will be lost.

The marbles might be used as a metaphor for the heaviness of the feelings our negative actions cause, or the weight and strength of positive feeling.

Getting Needs Met in Relationships

> **Resources required:** *Copies of Worksheet 34: Meeting Needs in Relationships – one per person*
>
> **Learning objectives:** *To develop students' awareness and understanding of their emotional needs and to appreciate how these needs are met through close relationships*

Share with the students the idea that having friendships and relationships helps others, and having a strong relationship with ourselves can get our needs met and helps us to meet the needs of others. Recap with students what we mean by our needs and how our needs can be both physical and emotional.

Ask students to think about what they might need from their closest friends and from others they spend time with – people they know in clubs or on sports teams, people they hang out with in their neighbourhood, siblings or cousins, etc. List some of the needs these people meet on the board, and as the facilitator, add some examples of your own. For instance:

My friend Sophie meets my needs for staying connected to my past (I met her when I was eight years old), keeps me grounded and real, and she allows me to offload all my problems because she knows me inside out. So:

Sophie– meets needs of connection; staying real; sharing problems.

Ask students to individually complete Worksheet 34: Meeting Needs in Relationships, and then come back together as a large group.

DISCUSSION POINTS

- *Did anyone notice they have different friends for different parts of their life or to meet different needs?*

- *Was it helpful to think specifically about what you need from your friends?*

- *Do we sometimes expect all things from all people?*

- *How often do we think about what our friends need from us?*

- *Did anyone identify any good strategies for strengthening their relationships?*

Facilitator notes

- Try to participate as much as you can in the discussions, giving examples from your own life about the different friends you have for different parts of your life, highlighting how you, too, have needs that people meet for you.

- It is important that students see you as a real person, too, and also understand that it's OK to have different types of friends: you don't just have to have a best friend.

Using 'I' Statements

Resources required: *Worksheet 35: 'I' Statement Cards – one set*

Copies of Worksheet 36: 'I' Statement Scenarios – one per person

Learning objectives: *To build a language of direct, open communication to ensure needs are met when building relationships and avoiding conflicts*

Ask the students to share some of the needs that their friends meet for them, identified in Activity 4.11: Getting Needs Met in Relationships, and write them on the board, e.g. 'fun, straight talking, honesty, respect, doing silly things and blowing off steam, keeping me focused on school work'.

Discuss with the students how our friends know what we need. Do we ask them directly to be honest or to respect us? Ask the students by a show of hands who would be likely to say to a friend, 'I'm feeling sad today, so I need to be left alone for a while to calm down and think things through.' Probably not many students would agree that this would be something they'd say! Discuss what the effect would be if we all communicated more directly like this.

Seat the students in a circle, and place the cut-up 'I' Statement Cards (Worksheet 35) in the middle, face up. Explain to students that they will choose an 'I' statement and complete the sentence, e.g. 'I feel angry when you…don't listen to me properly.' Provide an example by going first, and then ask the students to do the same, moving around the circle until everyone has had a go.

Discuss whether it was easy or difficult to read the 'I' statement aloud. Why? Share with students the three-part system for using 'I' statements to better communicate with others:

- Observe the situation and how you feel without blaming others.

- 'Own it' by using an 'I' statement, and communicate how you feel (so what you're saying is about you, not someone else).

- Ask for what you need (without demanding).

For example:

- Your friends are all talking excitedly about going to a party you haven't been invited to:

  ○ *Observe the situation and how you feel: They've been invited but I haven't; I feel left out, sad and frustrated that they're talking about it in front of me*

  ○ *Own it with an 'I' statement, and ask for what you need: 'I'm upset that I haven't been invited to the party, so I need you guys to change the subject.'*

Ask students individually to complete Worksheet 36: 'I' Statement Scenarios, considering how they can communicate more effectively in the given scenarios.

The Pressure is On!

Resources required:	*None*
Learning objectives:	*To define and understand peer pressure and to explore methods for managing situations of peer pressure*

Discuss what the term 'peer pressure' means. Peer pressure is the positive or negative influence of others that can make us engage in activities or behave in a certain way. We may know when we are experiencing peer pressure by the feeling that someone is pushing us towards a certain choice, good or bad. *Negative peer pressure is the unwanted pressure that causes a person to participate in activities that may hurt themselves or others, including creating emotional hurt.*

Ask the students to identify some examples of both positive and negative peer pressure and offer real examples they may have witnessed or experienced, if they feel comfortable to do so.

Explain to the students that peer pressure can be *spoken* or *unspoken*:

- *Spoken pressure* (direct): put-down (e.g. making a verbal comment or insult), reasoning (e.g. trying to persuade someone to do something).

- *Unspoken pressure* (indirect): dirty looks (e.g. a dirty look or a stare that implies a feeling of disgust or humour), rejection (e.g. leaving someone out), huddling together (e.g. a group standing together looking or laughing), creating an example (e.g. buying, wearing or doing something to set an example for others to follow).

Split students into three groups; one group should stand in the middle of the room – they will be deciding if they agree or disagree with the statements you read out. The second group should stand on the 'agree' side of the room, and the third group should stand on the 'disagree' side of the room.

The deciders will listen to the statements and move to the side of the room that corresponds to whether they feel they agree or disagree with the statement. The group on the 'agree' side will use *unspoken peer pressure tactics* to make them come to their side. The group on the 'disagree' side will use *spoken peer pressure tactics* to make them come to their side of the room.

Read the following list of statements, and ask the students in the middle group to move to the side of the room which corresponds to how they feel. The agree and disagree groups can start using their tactics as soon as you have read the statement, until everyone has decided where they should stand.

- Chocolate is better than candy.

- Going to school is important.

- Healthy food is better than junk food.

- Football is better than basketball.

- Reality TV shows are for idiots.

- A girl needs to have a boyfriend to be popular.

Discuss how it made the people feel who had to choose whether they would agree or disagree. Did anyone change their mind because of the spoken or unspoken peer pressure?

Now repeat the activity, moving people around so another group gets to stand in the middle. Explain that you will now read aloud some more serious situations. The group in the middle has to decide if they agree or disagree as before, with the two groups using the unspoken and spoken peer pressure tactics again.

- Your friend is being bullied by an older group of students; you should help them – agree or disagree?

- You just got told a rumour about someone you know and like; your friend is begging you to tell them what you heard. You should pass it on – agree or disagree?

- A group of popular kids are going to cut class for the last period. You should go with them – agree or disagree?

- A friend has set up a hate page on Facebook for one of your teachers; they're asking you to comment on the teacher. You should join in – agree or disagree?

DISCUSSION POINTS

- *How difficult was it to keep your own mind and to do what you felt was right when there was external pressure?*

- *Which was worse, the spoken or unspoken pressure?*

- *Did anyone surprise themselves and succumb to the pressure when they thought they'd be able to resist it?*

- *How did it feel to be someone who was pressurizing the group?*

- *Has anyone noticed that they've done this before, whether they meant to or not?*

Peer Pressure

Resources required: *Copies of Worksheet 37: Scenarios – one scenario card per group*

Learning objectives: *To define and understand peer pressure and explore methods for managing situations of peer pressure*

Recap on what is meant by the term 'peer pressure', and discuss ways in which people can use unspoken and spoken tactics to pressure someone in a negative way (as explored in Activity 4.13: The Pressure is On!).

Split the students into groups of about five or six, and ask one student to stand on a chair with the rest of the group standing around in a circle. The group must use peer pressure to make the student get off the chair. Give each group a scenario card from Worksheet 37: Scenarios, and ask each person around the student standing on the chair to say something to persuade her to go their way, taking turns to speak. If the student is swayed by the pressure, she should respond to each person in turn, by doing one of the following:

1. Crouching on the chair.

2. Sitting on the chair.

3. Standing next to the chair.

4. Sitting on the floor next to the chair.

5. Lying on the floor (this indicates the student has completely succumbed to the pressure).

If the student on the chair does not feel swayed by what is said to her, she should remain standing in her position.

When each person has had their turn, look around the room and see who is left crouching on their chair, sitting, standing next to their chair, and who is sitting or lying on the floor.

DISCUSSION POINTS

- *How difficult was it to stay standing?*

- *How do those people who ended up sitting on the floor feel? What made you give in at the end?*

- *How do those people feel who didn't give in and stayed standing or crouching on the chair?*

- *What tactics did those people use who stayed standing? What feeling are you left with?*

Concentric Circles
Concentric Circles in My Life

Consider all of the people in your life with whom you have some sort of relationship. There are all sorts of people that you know – some of whom may be really close to you, like your family, while others you might just know as an acquaintance.

Fill in the circles below with the people in your life by writing in their names or initials, starting with the people closest to you in the circle nearest 'me', and then the people next closest to you in the next circle, and so on. The people you know least, such as those who you know by sight or know just to say hello to, should go in the outer circle.

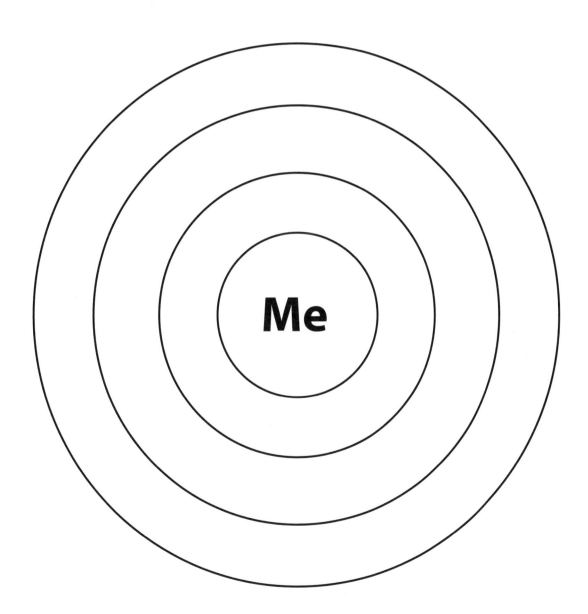

Friendship Agree/Disagree
Statements

Read the following statements aloud to students and ask them to decide whether they agree or disagree with the statement or they don't know, and 'vote with their feet'.

Statement 1

Not having a best friend is weird.

Statement 2

A friend should do everything you ask them to do.

Statement 3

It's good to have different friends for different parts of your life or interests.

Statement 4

Drama in friendship groups is normal and to be expected.

Statement 5

You should be able to count on a friend no matter what.

Statement 6

It's normal to fight with your friends and fall out.

Statement 7

I am a good friend to others.

Statement 8

I should be friendly to everyone I meet, even if they're not my 'friends'.

Statement 9

It's OK to spread gossip about a friend if you heard it from someone else and didn't start it.

Statement 10

Being a good friend takes work and effort.

Relationship Skills
Friendship Scenarios

Scenario 1

Rachel and Anna have always been best friends, ever since they were babies. When they moved up to high school together, Rachel started hanging out with some new people; she made friends easily and enjoyed spending time with a bigger group. Anna felt left out and hurt; she wanted to be best friends with Rachel like they used to be, always doing things together. Anna began to feel quite jealous and, without thinking it through, posted a comment about Rachel on Facebook for everyone to see. Other people commented and soon a huge group of people were laughing and making fun at Rachel, who was devastated and hurt. Anna felt embarrassed and sorry for her actions, but the damage had been done. Rachel didn't even want to talk to her, and now she had no friends at all.

Scenario 2

Claire has a big group of friends who hang out most days in school and on the weekends. The group gets along most of the time, but every now and then big arguments start which can go on for days and days. One person accuses another girl of doing or saying something behind her back, and the rest of the group take sides. Claire always feels stuck in the middle and frustrated. She doesn't want to get involved in all the drama, but she doesn't want to leave the group, either. She's afraid of saying anything in case she becomes a target for bullying by the rest of the group.

Scenario 3

Everyone thinks Jack, a boy a few years older, is really cute, especially Holly and her friends. Everyone knows he is the best looking boy in school, and when he asks Holly out on a date, she's overjoyed! Her friends, however, are not impressed. They accuse Holly of going off and leaving them for a boy and turning her back on them. Holly feels torn between her friends and her boyfriend. She wishes she could have both, but they say they won't talk to her until she dumps him.

Best Friends Forever
The BFF Quiz

Being a friend can sometimes be a tough job. Friends give us support, share fun times, care for us and listen when we need to have a good moan, but friendships can also be full of drama, arguments, gossip and backstabbing. *Being* a good friend is as important as choosing good friends. Take the BFF Quiz and see if you're a best friend forever or a frenemy.

1. Your best friend has just been asked out on a date by the hottest boy in school. You:

   a. Act excited for her and ask her to dish the goss, even though you're a bit jealous.

   b. Tell her he's seeing someone else and is a cheat and liar – you're protecting her in the long run, right?

2. You and your best friend have plans to go shopping all day on Saturday, but you've just been asked to go to a party with the coolest girls in your year. You:

   a. Ditch your friend by telling her you feel ill – she'll never find out.

   b. Tell the group of girls you can't make it till later.

3. Two girls in your friendship group are always making fun of another girl, laughing at her and giving her dirty looks. You:

   a. Tell them to stop – it's bullying and the girl is probably feeling miserable.

   b. Join in – if you say anything they might start on you.

4. You're at the coolest party ever when your dad turns up to tell you to go home – super embarrassing! Your friends:

   a. Snigger along with everyone else and pretend they don't know you.

   b. Tell you it doesn't matter, the party is practically over anyway.

5. Your close friend has failed her third test in a row. You:

   a. Offer to help tutor her and revise with her on the weekend.

   b. Distance yourself from her a bit – you don't want your grades going down too.

6. One of your friends is doing karaoke at a party and sounds *awful*! You:

   a. Jump up there quick and grab a mic to join in.

   b. Laugh along with everyone else.

7. Your best friend has just admitted to having a secret crush on the guy you like, too. You:

    a. Keep quiet and don't say anything about your feelings.

    b. Tell her you like him too and gossip about how hot he is.

8. A friend forwards you a text message with some gossip about another friend. You:

    a. Forward it on – you weren't the one who wrote it, and you didn't say it was true.

    b. Delete it and tell your other friend what's going on.

The BFF Test: The results!

Your score

Number of (a): ……………………

Number of (b): ……………………

If you scored four or more (a)s

Frenemy alert! There's a fine line between being a good friend and just going along with what everyone else is doing. Being a good friend takes work, effort and the ability to make good choices. There's an old saying that goes, 'with friends like that, who needs enemies!'

Tip: Try thinking about your *choices* before you make them. Imagine how your friend will feel and how you would feel if the situation were reversed.

If you scored four or more (b)s

Best Friend Forever! You think about your friends' feelings and you're not afraid to go against the crowd to be there for your friend. Your friends know they can trust you and rely on you to be there for them.

Tip: Don't forget to get your needs met, too. Being a good friend is important, but make sure your friends are also giving you the support and trust that you need. Relationships should be 50–50, with each person giving and taking.

Cliques
Clique Scenarios

Your group accepts that you have friends in different classes, in different clubs, and outside of school, and they're OK with that.

Your boyfriend dumps you publicly, and your friends rush to support you, telling you it will be OK.

Your boyfriend dumps you publicly, and everyone is laughing at you. Suddenly, your friends don't seem to want to hang out with you and avoid you in school.

You're trying out a new style and have accidently dyed your hair pink. Your friend lends you a hat and laughs it off with you.

Your group of friends tell you that you have to do certain things to be allowed to stay in the group, like make fun of that boy who's really shy and quiet.

Your friendship group wouldn't dream of talking to or sitting with the kids who hang out in the library, and you wouldn't even dare to suggest it for fear of what they'd say or do.

You befriend the new girl in school and find that your group suddenly aren't talking to you.

You have friends from your old school, your class, other schools, and your neighbourhood, and everyone's OK with that.

Your friends only invite you to go to certain places with them and restrict what you can see on their Facebook profiles, but deny it when you question them.

You know that even if you're having a really bad day and take it out on your friends, they'd understand and still be there for you.

You can't tell whether your friends are really friends at all – they blow so hot and cold all the time, you're never sure if you're doing or saying the right things to please them.

Kirsty saw you sitting on your own at lunch and invited you to join her table.

You're invited to a party by a group of girls in your year, but when you get there, they ignore you and act as though they've never even see you before.

Every time you look at Laura and her friends, they huddle together and whisper and giggle, looking in your direction.

A group of older girls ask if you want to join their game of volleyball.

Your friends say you can't hang around with them unless you change your clothes and style to be more like them.

You find out you've been de-friended by a group of girls in your class on Facebook, and you know they're talking about you on the site.

When playing football, the boys switch from team to team, depending on who's short, and ask students in lower years to join in if they want.

A group of girls always hang around in the park after school and in the evenings, intimidating people. They won't let anyone else use the park unless they smoke, drink and cause trouble like they do.

Your friends always come in to school wearing their hair the same way and with the same accessories. You never seem to be in on the secret the night before, and it makes you feel like the odd one out.

The most popular girl in school invites you to a party. All her group say they're going and are really excited. When you show up on Friday night, there is no one there. On Monday, they whisper and laugh whenever you walk in the room.

The Drama Triangle

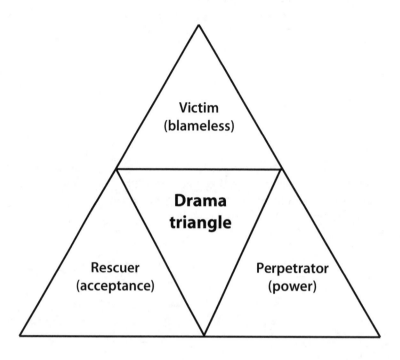

Think about and write down:

- Times when I am being a victim – what does this make me say? How does this make me act?

  _____

- Times when I am being a perpetrator – what does this make me say? How does this make me act?

  _____

- Times when I am being a rescuer – what does this make me say? How does this make me act?

  _____

- Which role do I take on most often? Why?

  _____

- How can I move away from playing this role?

  _____

Getting Needs Met in Relationships
Meeting Needs in Relationships

Name of friend	What do I need from this person?	What might this person need from me?	What else could I do to strengthen this relationship, so both our needs are met?
Example: Aaliyah	Good conversations Honesty To keep me grounded and real To remind me of where I came from	Support Positivity and encouragement Company To spend time with her	Make more of an effort to keep in touch Invite her to spend time with my other groups of friends

Using 'I' Statements
'I' Statement Cards

I feel angry when…	I feel hurt when…	I don't like it when you…
I am in control of myself when…	I feel secure when…	I feel uncomfortable when you…
I am at my best when I…	I am a good person because…	I am a good friend when I…
I need my friends to…	I need some time alone when…	I struggle to be friends with you when…

I find it hard to be myself when…

I am at my happiest when…

I feel listened to when…

I feel respected when…

I feel unsure of myself when…

I need to be around others when…

I can't be around you when…

I need support when…

I feel lonely when…

I feel sad when…

I need help when…

I love being me when…

Using 'I' Statements
'I' Statement Scenarios

Scenario: what happened	Observe the situation and how you feel	Own it with an 'I' statement and ask for what you need: 'I………'
Example: Your friends are all talking excitedly about going to a party you haven't been invited to.	*They've been invited, but I haven't; I feel left out, sad, and frustrated that they're talking about it in front of me.*	*'I'm upset that I haven't been invited to the party, so I need for you guys to change the subject.'*
Your best friend has just started dating the boy you really like, and can't stop talking about him.		
Your friendship group are bullying someone in the year below. She's a girl you like and hang out with outside of school.		
Your friends are making fun of you and calling you a wimp for not wanting to skip school and go smoking in the park with older kids.		
Your two best friends keep getting into big arguments, causing a rift in your group, and making everyone take sides.		

Peer Pressure
Scenarios

Scenario 1

The girl in the middle is between two groups of friends who are having a huge argument. Your group think that the others have been spreading vicious rumours across the school about all of you. You want her to come over to your side and stop speaking to them and hanging out with them. They are the enemy! Try to encourage her to distance herself from this other group.

Scenario 2

Your group are bullying a girl in another class. She thinks she's really amazing and loves herself, so she's got it coming to her! The girl in the middle doesn't agree with you, and won't join in the bullying. She's making you feel a bit guilty about what you've been doing, and that's no good! Try to make her see sense and join in.

Scenario 3

Your group have heard that some girls from another school have been spreading gossip about you all, and a big fight is brewing. The girl in the middle is not into fighting and is threatening to tell the teacher, saying that it would be the best for everyone. These girls need to be taught a lesson, and you need her on board. Try to persuade her to keep quiet.

Theme 5

Conflict Resolution

Responding to Conflict 1

Resources required: *Copies of Worksheet 38: Scenario and Actions – one per small group*

Learning objective: *To explore our responses to conflict*

As a whole group, discuss what conflict is and ensure that the students have a good understanding of the range of conflicts, from a small disagreement to an argument, a fight, or even a war!

Place students into small groups, and hand each group a copy of Worksheet 38: Scenario and Actions. Ask students to decide which action they would take if they were in each scenario. Some members of the group may have different ideas about which action to take, and so a compromise might need to be made.

Ask each group to feed back their answers and discuss any differences in opinions.

DISCUSSION POINTS

- *What are the consequences of the actions you chose?*

- *Which actions are passive, which are aggressive, and which are assertive?*

Conflict Triangle

Resources required: *Copies of Worksheet 39: Conflict Triangles 1 and 2 – one per person*

Learning objectives: *To build students' awareness of the consequences to conflict and to consider alternative actions to take*

Ask the students to consider a time when they caused a conflict at school or at home. Using Worksheet 39: Conflict Triangles 1 and 2, students should individually describe the conflict, what the consequences were, and how their actions made people feel. Students should then repeat the activity, this time considering what they could have done to avoid the conflict, what the consequences then would have been, and how they and others would have felt.

DISCUSSION POINTS

- *Is it easy to avoid conflict or to choose a different action to avoid it?*

- *How does it make you feel when you avoid conflict or choose to let something go?*

- *If it makes us feel better when we don't argue or fight with someone we care about, why do we do it?*

Activity 5.3
Chains of Conflict

Resources required: *Strips of paper to make paper chains – one set of strips per person*

Pens

Sticky tape

Learning objective: *To explore how we choose our friends and why*

Each student should make a paper chain to represent all the conflicts they have had this past week, including conflicts at home, in school, with friends, or with themselves (an internal conflict). Label each loop of the chain in pen so it represents one conflict. When everyone is ready, explain that students must link their chains to anyone else's in the room they've ever had a conflict with. Students will need to make extra loops to stretch out their chain to meet other people's. In the end, one big mess of paper chains will be created!

Discuss how our conflicts connect us, and how we've created a web of conflict across the room.

DISCUSSION POINTS

- *What do these chains represent, in terms of feelings and consequences?*

- *How different would our lives be if these chains represented positivity and friendship?*

- *Can our arguments and fights sometimes leave us feeling as though we're in chains?*

- *Some people's conflicts can last a lifetime, such as a family feud that separates people for years. How would that feel? Can it be avoided?*

Box of Conflict

Resources required: *Small cardboard boxes or a box template on cards – one per person*

Scissors

Marker pens

Magazines and newspapers

Sticky tape

Glue sticks

Sheets of paper

Learning objective: *To understand how our external actions can differ from our internal thoughts*

Give each student a small cardboard box. These can be collected from local scrap stores, recycled from grocery stores, brought in by the students, or created using a printed template on thick card that students can cut out and tape to form a cubed box.

Provide students with some magazines, newspapers and marker pens, and explain that each student is making a box to represent a conflict. Students should decorate the outside of the box with words, phrases and images that describe what happens in the moment of conflict, such as the heat of an argument or the middle of a fight. Inside the box, students can cut out and paste, or draw images, words, phrases or patterns to represent their true thoughts and feelings during or after the moment of conflict. For example, they may feel hurt, regretful, ashamed or confused.

DISCUSSION POINTS

- *What would happen if we turned the box inside out and showed people our true feelings instead?*

- *Why do we say or do those things in the moment of conflict?*

- *How did it feel to create your box? Was anyone surprised by their feelings inside?*

- *When our actions don't match up with our feelings, do we create conflict inside ourselves? (For example, getting into a physical fight when we really want to tell someone they hurt our feelings.)*

Feelings Detective

> **Resources required:** *Copies of Worksheet 40: Scenarios – one per person or one per small group*
>
> **Learning objective:** *To develop students' awareness of how to communicate more effectively, using 'I' statements to own their feelings*

Discuss with the group of students how people in conflict rarely say what they really mean and rarely get their thoughts and feelings across in the most effective way. Screaming 'It's so unfair' at your parents might really mean 'I'm so frustrated I can't go out tonight, because all my friends are going and I feel left out and babyish.'

Ask students to work individually or in small groups to read Worksheet 40: Scenarios, and to try to guess what feeling the person is trying to communicate (e.g. angry, sad, hurt, frustrated), and what they are really trying to say, which would avoid conflict (starts with 'I').

DISCUSSION POINTS

- *Why don't we say what we really feel?*

- *How would your parents, teacher or friend respond if you calmly told them how you felt, instead of shouting your feelings?*

Responding to Conflict 2

Resources required: *Copies of Worksheet 41: Our Responses to Conflict Action Cards – one set per pair*

Copies of Worksheet 42: Scenarios – one worksheet per pair

Learning objectives: *To identify appropriate means of responding to conflict, to understand how to prevent conflict from escalating, and to apply conflict resolution skills to real-life situations*

Display and discuss as a group the four different means for responding to conflict: ignore, avoid, deflect and confront. Ask the group to list examples of actions they might take under each of the categories. For examples see below.

Ignore Don't talk to them; leave the friendship group	**Avoid** Walk away; stay away from class; take a different route to school
Deflect Cause arguments with other friends; bring others into the arguments; convince other friends to resolve the problem	**Confront** Argue; fight

Facilitator notes

- The four words ignore, avoid, deflect and confront should be displayed clearly to assist the group when completing Worksheet 42: Scenarios.

Explain to the group that we can use all four strategies at once or select the one we feel will most effectively resolve the conflict. Working in pairs, ask the group to reflect on a time when they may have used one or more of these strategies. Ask them to consider if their strategy was successful in resolving the conflict. When feeding back to the group their discussions, consider reflecting on the reasons they felt their strategy did not work. Distribute Worksheet 41: Our Responses to Conflict Action Cards and Worksheet 42: Scenarios (one each per pair). Ask students to work in their pairs to match up each scenario with an action card, and feed back discussion to the group as a whole. In pairs, match up each scenario with an action card, and feed back discussion to the group as a whole.

DISCUSSION POINTS

- *How do we learn to resolve conflict?*

- *Are we aware of the strategies we use to resolve conflict or are our responses automatic?*

- *Do our feelings and thoughts affect how we resolve conflict?*

Facilitator notes

- This activity not only outlines strategies for resolving conflict, but also explores how we chose the strategies we use to resolve conflict. When introducing Worksheet 42: Scenarios, it is important that you reflect on the thoughts and feelings that drive our responses to conflict.

Media Conflicts

Resources required:	*Copies of teen, celebrity or current affairs magazines*
	Large sheets of paper
	Marker pens
Learning objectives:	*To explore the impact of conflict in our culture and society, to build awareness of the effects of conflict, to develop discernment and equality of thinking to view both sides of a dispute, and to build empathy and understanding for others*

Discuss with the students how often we see or hear about conflicts on a day-to-day basis. Examples of conflict are everywhere – in our homes, schools, communities, on TV, in far-off places, in our country, in magazines and music. Conflict is natural and to be expected, but it is how we deal with it that counts.

Spilt the students into groups of four or five. Give each group a copy of a teen, celebrity or current affairs magazine which has suitable examples of real-life stories. You could use the Internet to find these instead if you don't have enough magazines to distribute equally.

Ask each group to find one example of a conflict happening in someone's life, and using a sheet of paper, write down as much information as they can find about the conflict.

Write the following points on the board to help students:

- How does the person feel?

- Who else is involved?

- Whose side are you hearing?

- What might be the other side?

- How do you think the people involved feel about their conflict being in the magazine?

- How could they have resolved the conflict?

- What words come to mind when you read the story?

- How could they have avoided this conflict?

When each group has finished, ask them to present the story and their notes.

Discuss as a whole group why the magazine chose to print the story.

- Do we enjoy reading about other people's pain and difficulties?

- Why?

Who's Right, Who's Wrong?

Resources required: *Copies of Worksheet 43: Who's Right? Scenarios – one scenario per pair*

Learning objectives: *To develop students' critical thinking and debating skills, and to understand the opposing thoughts, feelings and viewpoints of parties involved*

Share with the students that there are always two sides to every story, and it can often be hard as a teacher or parent to work out who is right and who is wrong. Sometimes this is near impossible!

Remind students about the situations they read about in the magazines during Activity 5.7: Media Conflicts – they were hearing one person's side. Did the story lean towards supporting that person, or did it give a balanced view? More than likely it was in favour of one person over the other, trying to sway the reader to believe one person was in the right and the other in the wrong.

Split the students into pairs and give each pair one scenario (Worksheet 43: Who's Right? Scenarios). Each pair has ten minutes to practise role playing their scenario, before they present to the rest of the group.

Give each pair time to act out their scenario. The rest of the group will be the audience and will take the role as written on the scenario (e.g. teacher, friend, parent, police officer). The audience must decide who is in the right and who is in the wrong, after they have seen the scenario acted out.

When each group has acted out their scenarios, discuss the following points:

DISCUSSION POINTS

- *How easy or hard was it to decide who was right and who was wrong?*

- *How do we know for certain that we got it right?*

- *Is anyone ever truly right or completely in the wrong, or is it all a matter of perception and how we view the situation?*

- *How does this change the way you think about teachers' jobs?*

Who's Affected?

Resources required:	*Copies of Worksheet 44: Scenarios – one scenario per small group*
	Large sheets of paper
	Marker pens
Learning objective:	*To develop awareness of the wider impact of conflict*

Ask the students to consider how many people are affected by a conflict. Identify some examples of conflict, write them on the board, and list the people who may be affected by or involved in the conflict. For example:

- Parents arguing – children affected; neighbours; police if conflict gets out of control.

- Two friends falling out over a boy – others in the friendship group; classmates; the boy; his friends; teachers.

- Two nations at war – citizens of both nations, politicians, armies and other military personnel; possibly the United Nations and other countries who intervene; families of people in those nations.

Discuss how the web of who is affected by conflict can be huge, as in the last example. What are the effects of this? Is it good to be involved in someone else's conflict?

Split students into groups of four to six, and give each group a large sheet of paper and marker pens. Give each group one of the scenarios contained on Worksheet 44: Scenarios. The group should consider who could possibly be affected by this conflict, writing the brief scenario in the middle of their sheet of paper and drawing an arrow to the name or type of person who could be affected.

When completed, ask each group to show their papers and briefly highlight who they thought might be affected and how.

DISCUSSION POINTS

- *Was anyone surprised by how far a conflict actually spread and how many people were affected?*

- *What are the consequences for all these people affected by the conflict?*

- *Why does so much conflict spread in this world instead of positivity, care and support for one another?*

Mediation Moguls

Resources required: *None required*

Learning objectives: *To practise skills and strategies to diffuse and manage situations of conflict, and to remain neutral and impartial*

As an ice breaker, play the game of Human Knots. Stand students in a circle (or if you have a large group, split into two or three circles). Each person must grab someone's right hand with their left hand and someone else's left hand with their right, so the group is well and truly tangled. The group has to untangle themselves back into a circle (or as near as possible!) without letting go or breaking hands.

Congratulate any groups who managed to untangle themselves, and ask what strategies they used to do it, for example, teamwork, someone taking charge, listening, one person speaking at a time. Discuss with students how we can sometimes get tangled up in other people's conflicts without meaning to, and it can feel like the human knot! A good way to help our friends through conflicts is to be a mediator rather than getting involved or taking sides.

A mediator is someone who helps two people or parties to talk about their views and feelings without taking sides, so that a common agreement or way forward can be reached. Stress to students that mediation isn't always about finding a perfect solution, or finding the truth – there may not be either! For example, two friends who have fallen out may decide it's better to stay away from each other than pretend to make up.

Write the following mediator's strategy on the board:

1. Ask Person A what happened and how they feel.

2. Ask Person B what happened and how they feel.

3. Ask Person A what they need to be able to move forward.

4. Ask Person B what they need to be able to move forward.

5. Ask both people what will happen next, and ask them to agree to stick to it.

Split the students into groups of three, and give each group some time to think of a conflict scenario. One person should be the mediator, and the other two should be in conflict. The mediator should go through the strategy on the board, taking time to gather information and focus on each person's thoughts and feelings. Make sure that all students know that the ground rules apply, and the two people in conflict cannot interrupt one another as they are having their turn to speak.

Repeat the activity twice so that each person in the trio has had a chance to be the mediator.

Discuss how it felt to be the mediator and the person receiving mediation.

- Did anyone feel heard and listened to?

- Did anyone feel they came out with a good way forward at the end of their mediation?

Responding to Conflict 1
Scenario and Actions

Scenario

Fatima has been best friends with Jess since they were really young. They recently moved up to high school and have been placed in different classes. Jess has become good friends with two of the girls in her class and has found she has a lot in common with them. Fatima has noticed that Jess has been hanging out with these girls more often during school and in the evenings, and she has not been invited to join them. Fatima is upset that Jess has been excluding her. At lunchtime one day, Fatima finds Jess to ask her if she wants to do something on the weekend. Jess responds that she has already made plans with her new friends. Fatima gets angry at this and starts to shout at Jess.

Imagine you are Jess, using the workspace below, discuss with your partner each strategy and list what your actions would be.

Strategy	What would Jess's actions be if she was feeling angry and thinking 'Why can't Fatima just leave me alone, I don't like her any more?'	What would Jess's actions be if she was feeling empathy towards Fatima and thinking 'I like Fatima as a person, but we have grown apart and do not have the same interests any more.'
Ignore		
Avoid		
Deflect		
Confront		

Conflict Triangle
Conflict Triangles 1 and 2

Think about a conflict at home or school. Complete Triangle 1, then complete Triangle 2.

1. Describe the conflict:

1. Describe the conflict:

1

2

3. How it made people feel:

2. What were the consequences?

3. How would others have felt if you had avoided it?

2. What could you have done to avoid the conflict?

Feelings Detective
Scenarios

Scenario: what happened	What feeling might they be trying to communicate?	What they are really trying to say: 'I… '
Your friend says: 'You're not interested in us now you're dating that boy. You're so fake!'		
Your dad says: 'You're not going out tonight after you came in so late last weekend. You're grounded, young lady!'		
Your best friend says: 'I can't believe you spread that rumour about me to everyone. I don't want to know you any more.'		
Your best friend says: 'That new haircut looks really stupid on you.'		
Your teacher says: 'How dare you talk in my class! Get out!'		

Responding to Conflict 2
Our Responses to Conflict Action Cards

Ignore	Say something back	Physically attack (e.g. kick, punch, slap)
Say how you feel	Go and get help	Tell someone you trust about it
Get some advice	Retaliate by doing the same thing back	Get your friends to gang up on them
Cry	Shrug it off and forget about it	Scream and shout
Join in and get involved with the conflict	Calmly ask them to stop	Walk away

Responding to Conflict 2
Scenarios

1. Your parents are having a huge argument, shouting and screaming downstairs. Your little brother is crying.

2. Your two best friends are arguing and both want you to take their side and ignore the other person.

3. Two people in the year above you are having a fight in the corridor. Everyone is standing around chanting and filming it on their phones.

4. Your boyfriend has just told you he can't go out with you tonight, and to stop calling and hassling him all the time.

Who's Right, Who's Wrong?
Who's Right? Scenarios

Scenario 1 – Person A

A girl in your year, Mia, has told you that a nasty rumour is going around the whole school about you. Mia said she heard it from your best friend (Person B) and she thinks it was her who spread it in the first place! You're absolutely furious. You can't believe your friend would do this to you. You haven't spoken to her since Mia told you.

Scenario 1 – Person B

Your best friend (Person A) is accusing you of spreading a rumour about her. A girl in your year, Mia, told her that you said it and now neither of them are talking to you. You swear you didn't say it, and Mia is making things up to try and come between you two. You're so angry that Mia did this and that your friend took her word over yours.

Scenario 2 – Person A

You and your friends thought it would be funny to set up a group on Facebook about one of your teachers. It all got out of hand, and people started posting horrible comments about the teacher on there. The school found out, and now you're all in big trouble. Your friend (Person B) is saying it was all your idea and trying to make you take the punishment for it. It caused a big argument and you two ended up having a fight.

Scenario 2 – Person B

You and your friends thought it would be funny to set up a group on Facebook about one of your teachers. It all got out of hand, and people started posting horrible comments about the teacher on there. The school found out, and now you're all in big trouble. It wasn't your idea, and you weren't really involved, but now your friend (Person A) is in trouble and is trying to drag you down with her. You told the teachers it was her, which caused a big fight between you.

Scenario 3 – Person A

Your friend (Person B) just started dating a boy a few years older than you. She is spending every minute with him – you hardly see her anymore! You think he's controlling and the relationship isn't healthy for her, and have tried to tell her he's no good and to dump him. She got really mad at this and hasn't spoken to you since.

Scenario 3 – Person B

You've just started dating this gorgeous boy who you really liked for ages. You couldn't believe your luck when he asked you out! But now you're friend is being super jealous and keeps saying stuff about him and trying to get you to dump him. It's obvious she's just jealous and wants him for herself. You're so mad you're not even talking to her right now.

Scenario 1

James doesn't really like school and skips quite a lot. He's falling behind in his school work, and he feels as though his teachers are out to get him. His mother works two jobs and his dad walked out last year, which makes James feel really angry. He has two younger brothers that he always ends up having to take care of, which he resents. Lately James has started going around with an older group of boys. They hang around the park and sometimes some of the boys like to cause trouble by throwing eggs or vandalizing cars. Darren and Mike, the main leaders of the group, told James that if he wants to stay in their gang he has to prove himself. There's a community centre near the school that the boys have all been banned from because they've caused so much trouble there. Darren and Mike have decided they're going to show the centre a lesson and set fire to it one night. James is really worried and doesn't want to be involved. He used to go the centre all the time to hang out after school, plus his mother's friend works there, but he really wants to be in the gang. If he's not in the gang, what else has he got?

James goes along with the plan and one night joins Mike and Darren at the centre. They climb in through a window at the back and start a fire. Suddenly, they hear police sirens. Mike and Darren have disappeared, but James is confused in the dark and can't find his way out. Before he knows what's happening, he's being dragged out by the police and is under arrest.

Scenario 2

Claire and her group of friends have a really up-and-down relationship. Sometimes everyone gets along really well, and then something can happen and everyone is arguing and taking sides. A rumour started around school that Tia and Melissa have been talking about Claire behind her back, saying that she's done things with boys and is easy. Suddenly, everyone in school seems to know about it. Claire is so angry that she decides to take revenge. She waits outside school and pounces on Melissa, pushing her to the floor and punching her. Melissa falls awkwardly and bangs her head on the concrete. Students from other year groups are gathered around Melissa who isn't moving. Some teachers run out and pull Claire off Melissa, calling an ambulance. Claire is sent home from school and her parents are called. Melissa has a concussion and is going to be off school for at least a week.

Scenario 3

Donna and her friends Maria and Michelle really hate their art teacher, Mrs Smith. They think she has it in for them and is always hard on them, putting them in detention when they've forgotten their homework and shouting at them all the time. They're sure that no one in the school likes her and she needs to be taught a lesson. One afternoon, the girls decide that they'll set up a Facebook page about Mrs Smith, and they start commenting about how horrible she is. They invite their friends to comment too, and before long the page is full of hateful and mean comments about the teacher.

A few days later, Donna, Maria and Michelle are called into the school office. The Facebook page was discovered, and they are in big trouble. Their parents are there and are very, very angry. They find out that Mrs Smith was so upset she's had to take time off work. Her husband has just lost his job as well, to add to her problems, and now she feels as though all the students in school hate her.

Index of Activities by Topic

The activities included in *Surviving Girlhood* can be used as stand-alone resources, for students with an identified need, in character education or health classes, for after-school programmes, and more. The activities are categorized by topic, but all activities are designed to develop students' self-awareness, critical thinking skills and emotional literacy.

Topic: Needs

Activity

Topic: Values

Activity

Topic: Emotional Literacy

Activity

Topic: Self-Esteem

Activity

Topic: Relationships

Activity

Topic: Identity

Activity

Topic: Media Literacy

Activity

Topic: Respect

Activity

Topic: Stereotypes
Activity

Topic: Self-Awareness
Activity

Topic: Responsibilities
Activity

Topic: Behaviour Management
Activity

Topic: Self-Regulation
Activity

Topic: Communication
Activity

Topic: Rights
Activity

References

American Psychological Association (2010) *Report of the APA Task Force on the Sexualization of Girls.* Washington, DC: APA. Accessed at http://www.apa.org/pi/women/programs/girls/report.aspx?item=2 on 22 May 2011.

Anderson, C.A., Sakamoto, A., Gentile, D.A., Ihoro, N., *et al.* (2008) 'Longitudinal effects of violent video games on aggression in Japan and the United States.' *Pediatrics 122*, 5, e1067–e1072.

Bandura, A. (1976) *Social Learning Theory.* Englewood Cliffs, NJ: Prentice Hall.

Beck, A. (1970) 'Cognitive therapy: Nature and relation to behavior therapy.' *Behavior Therapy 1*, 2, 184–200.

Berndt, T. (1982) 'The features and effects of friendship in early adolescence.' *Child Development 53*, 6, 1447–1460.

Berne, E. (1964) *Games People Play: The Psychology of Human Relationships.* New York: Grove Press.

Brown, M.L. (2003) *Girlfighting: Betrayal and Rejection among Girls.* New York: New York University Press.

Brown, M.L. and Gilligan, C. (1992) *Meeting at the Crossroads: Women's Psychology and Girls' Development.* Cambridge, MA: Harvard University Press.

Craig, W. and Pepler, D. (1997) 'Observations of bullying and victimization in the school yard.' *Canadian Journal of School Psychology 13*, 2, 41–59.

Csikszentmihályi, M. (2002) *Flow: The Classic Work on How to Achieve Happiness.* London: Rider.

Department for Children, Schools and Families (2009) *Safe to Learn: Embedding Anti-bullying Work in School: Guidance for Schools on Preventing and Responding to Sexist, Sexual and Transphobic Bullying.* Nottingham: DCSF.

Erikson, E. (1968) *Identity, Youth and Crisis.* London: Norton.

Erikson, E. (1995) *Childhood and Society.* London: Vintage. (Original work published 1950.)

Ernst, F., Jr. (1971) 'The OK corral: The grid for get-on-with.' *Transactional Analysis Journal 1*, 4, 33–42.

Intersperience Research (2011) *Scoring Friends.* Milnthorpe, Cumbria: Intersperience. Accessed at www.intersperience.com/article_more.asp?art_id=49&current_id=1 on 23 May 2012.

Jack, D.C. (1993) *Silencing the Self: Women and Depression.* Cambridge, MA: Harvard University Press.

Kaiser Family Foundation (2010) *GENERATION M2 Media in the Lives of 8- to 18-Year-Olds.* Menlo Park, CA: Kaiser Family Foundation. Accessed at www.kff.org/entmedia/mh012010pkg.cfm on 21 July 2011.

Karpman, S. (1968) 'Fairy tales and script drama analysis.' *Transactional Analysis Bulletin 7*, 26, 39–43.

Maslow, A. (1943) 'A theory of human motivation.' *Psychological Review 50*, 4, 370–396.

Nadeau, J. (1992) 'Differential relations of parental acceptance and marital harmony to boys' and girls' friendships.' Thesis. Department of psychology, Concordia University, Montreal, Canada.

Olweus, D. (1973) 'Personality and Aggression.' In J.K. Coie and D.D. Jensen (eds) *Nebraska Symposium on Motivation.* Lincoln, NE: University of Nebraska Press.

Olweus, D. (1978) *Aggression in the Schools: Bullies and Whipping Boys.* New York: Wiley.

Rosenberg, M.B. (2003) *Nonviolent Communication: A Language of Life.* Encinitas, CA: Puddledancer Press.

Rosenburg, F. and Simmons, R. (1975) 'Sex differences in the self-concept in adolescence.' *Sex Roles 1*, 2, 147–159.

Seligman, M. (2007) *The Optimistic Child: A Proven Program to Safeguard Children Against Depression and Build Lifelong Resilience.* Boston, MA: Houghton Mifflin.

The New York Times (2007) Yankelovich Consumer Research. New York, NY. Accessed at http://www.nytimes.com/2007/01/15/business/media/15everywhere.html?pagewanted=al/ on 13 February 2011.